Treasury
of
American Music
Lesson Plans

Treasury
of
American Music
Lesson Plans

MARCELLE VERNAZZA

PARKER PUBLISHING COMPANY, INC.

WEST NYACK, NEW YORK

© 1980 by

PARKER PUBLISHING COMPANY, INC.

West Nyack, New York

Library of Congress Cataloging in Publication Data

Vernazza, Marcelle
  Treasury of American music lesson plans.

  Includes index.
  1. School music—United States—Instruction and
study.   2. Music, American—Instruction and study.
I. Title
MT3.U5V47   780′.7′2973   79-26855
ISBN 0-13-930651-X

Printed in the United States of America

Dedicated to the memory of my parents,
proud Kentuckians,
William Ira Wynn and Emeline Browles Wynn

I wish to acknowledge the help and encouragement given me by Sister Mary Dominic Ray, O.P., Founder and Director of the American Music Research Center, Dominican College, San Rafael, California.

What This Book Will Do For You

Developing Music Skills With American Music

American music is rich in its variety of styles, performance media, interest level for different age groups, and degrees of sophistication. *Treasury of American Music Lesson Plans* uses American music to involve students in music and motivate them to learn the basic elements of music. It develops music skills such as (1) singing many different kinds of songs, (2) playing American instruments, (3) listening to a variety of music composed and performed by Americans, (4) dancing and playing American singing games, and (5) acquiring skills needed to create their own American music.

Lessons are planned for specific grades according to the levels of interest and abilities. Each lesson plan focuses on one facet of music, yet does not neglect related elements of music. Materials needed for the lessons are classroom instruments and other things generally available to teachers. These are always listed. Background information to help you prepare the lesson has been researched and condensed for your use. To help you further, a sequence for presentation is included. This is a plan for a full lesson, one that you may follow exactly or vary according to your own background and the needs of your students.

Part One is **Singing American Music.** It includes songs of interest for each grade level, songs from different periods of American history and different parts of the country, easy songs and songs to challenge the talented student, songs typically American and songs that preserve ethnic heritages.

Part Two is **Playing American Instruments.** There are lessons on playing instruments that are uniquely American, like the ukulele and the dulcimer, as well as other instruments that Americans have adopted as their own like the guitar, recorder, and certain percussion instruments. These lessons teach performance skills, are actively related to other parts of the book and can be used with songs, dances, and for composition.

Part Three is **Listening to American Music.** The lessons in this part are designed not only to build up an appreciation of American music but to stimulate involvement in music. As an example, listening to Joplin's "Maple Leaf Rag" involves identifying the ragged rhythm of the treble, the basic beat of the bass and the sequence of the parts. Suggestions for enrichment include exploring the rhythm with movement, analyzing the notation, and comparing ragtime to other forms of dance music. There are lesson plans presenting many kinds of music from each century of American music.

Part Four is **Moving to American Music.** The lesson plans include both patterned and creative movement. For example, there are singing games, beginning line, circle, and square dances, and dramatizations with movement.

Part Five is **Creating American Music.** This includes material such as a lesson for young children—creating musical fragments for the moment, a plan to help fourth graders make up a hula, or suggestions for composing a rondo or creating original blues. These lesson plans are especially designed to stimulate and encourage the creative processes of young Americans making music.

Through the contributions of many kinds of people from many different places, America has developed a musical culture of its own. *Treasury of American Music Lesson Plans* gives teachers the opportunity to bring the study of this culture into the classroom. With the many demands on your time, you may not be able to do the necessary research or prepare the step-by-step lesson plans. This book will help you. Here you will find lesson plans for a great variety of American music from kindergarten through eighth grade.

The Heritage of American Music

American music reflects the music of the world's people, from Europe, Africa, the Orient, Central and South America. Through the amalgamation of many backgrounds, American music has established itself as a major body of literature with many styles and functions, and every basic element of music.

Rhythms range from the simple beat of the tune, "Go Tell Aunt Rhody" through Sousa marches, to the jazz rhythms of Gershwin and the sophisticated treatment of electronic sounds. *Melodies* include standard folk songs like "The Riddle" and "The Old Woman and Her Pig," Indian chants, rousing melodies from musicals like *Oklahoma,* and new sounds from the synthesizer. *Harmonies* range from the easy round, "I'm Gonna' Leave Old Texas Now" to symphonic Americana.

It's all here, researched, organized and sequenced into easy-to-use lesson plans for your particular grade level. Using these lessons, your students will have an opportunity to explore, understand, and participate in their heritage of American music.

American music is folk music – native American, European in many traditions, provincial, following the Western movement, war and protest, work songs, love, family, play. You will find lesson plans for much of this music.

Alaska's Eskimos, Indians from the Northwest to the Everglades of Florida, and the Polynesians in Hawaii offer their musical contributions. Europeans from England, Sweden, Germany, Italy, and other countries brought their folk ballads, peasant and court dances, and children's play games. From Africa came half-remembered tribal traditions that have not only been kept alive but have developed into the jazz idiom, perhaps the most American of music.

The early isolated settlements of the Appalachian Mountains, around the lakes in Minnesota, and in the open spaces of Texas, preserved some of their ethnic music and added ballads describing their own lives and times. The covered wagon trains, the cowboys and the California gold seekers sang and danced to lighten the hardships of pioneering and hard work. Each war brought songs of revolution, separation, protest, sadness of departure and death, and joy of reunion. Through it all, children played and sang in their own way, reflecting their heritage and what was happening.

American music is religious music – rituals, spirituals, revival and gospel songs, choir music, adaptations from the Far Eastern religions, traditional masses from Europe.

The rituals and religious chants of American Indians, with their own tonal and rhythmic systems, sounded strange to ears accustomed to the diatonicism of European music. But it was not long before these new Americans produced *The Bay Psalm Book* (1640), designed to help improve congregational singing. William Billings wrote new American hymns. African Americans created spirituals to express their Christianity. In the nineteenth century, people sang gospel hymns and, with the traveling tent and revival meetings, developed a religious fervor expressed only in that brand of hymnody. The modal music of the Roman Catholic mass endured and paralleled the gospel songs.

American music is light entertainment music – transplanted European dances, eighteenth and nineteenth century ballads, ragtime, tin pan alley songs, jazz, popular songs, country and, finally, the rock beat. You will find lesson plans using many different kinds of this ever-changing music.

This kind of music, always matching the temperament of the times, represents the recreational part of America. Even the first settlers took time to sing, and sometimes to dance, modifying European steps to fit the place, even if it happened to be the dirt floor of a log cabin or a newly raised barn. Ballad singing, evening entertainment around the fire, re-told tales, and records of life as it happened are all important parts of American music.

Stephen Foster blended folk and popular idioms in his songs. Ragtime, saddling the nineteenth and twentieth centuries, broke down some of the rigid, narrow musical ideas and set Americans and the new millions from Europe dancing and whistling.

The songs of the 1920s led to the popular songs that helped Americans through the great depression of the 1930s. The swing era led to progressive jazz which blended into maverick forms, and eventually into rock. It is important for children to understand and know about these developments. You will find lesson plans for entertainment music in this book.

American music is concert and recital music – at first only parlor music imported from Europe, then vocal and instrumental solo recitals, musical theatre, symphony, band and choral groups. As soon as the earliest settlers had time to rest, they began to think of cultural concerns. The ballad opera emerged as the first kind of musical theater.

The more privileged began to look for a traveling music "Professor" to teach their children. Louis Gottschalk of

Louisiana fused the music of the Caribbean and the negroes of the South into the popular "Bamboula." Scott Joplin, who had made himself "King of Ragtime," composed an opera *Treemonisha* and began to think of giving concerts instead of playing in clubs. Edward McDowell composed a new kind of American music with a slightly German accent.

The background materials in the lesson plans will help you present this kind of music to your students.

American music is part of education – the rural singing school, instrumental and vocal music in the public schools, community bands, orchestras, ensembles and chorales, the ever-changing styles in children's music, conservatory and college training in theory and performance.

The singing school of the nineteenth century was at once a neighborhood music school, a social institution, and a choir training program. Lowell Mason of Boston was the first to teach vocal music in a public school. In the twentieth century, children play in school bands and orchestras and sing in choruses. Adults continue this in community ensembles. Conservatories and universities offer degrees in music and prepare students to be performers, teachers, amateur musicians and concertgoers.

Here you will find lessons discussing the singing schools and the shaped notes they used, American instrumental innovations like the dulcimer and the ukulele, and other facets of music in education.

American music is all of these things and more. It is a heritage. Using these lesson plans, your students will sing the songs, dance the dances, play the instruments, listen to the concert and light entertainment numbers and make up their own American music.

Marcelle Vernazza

Contents

Part One: Singing American Music

Part Two: Playing American Instruments

Part Three: Listening to American Music

Lesson Title	Grades
Banshee by Henry Cowell	3 – 8
Prelude II by George Gershwin	4 – 8
Largo from *Evocations* by Carl Ruggles	4 – 8
Show Boat by Kern and Hammerstein	7 – 8
Oklahoma by Rodgers and Hammerstein	4 – 8
Put on a Happy Face from *Bye Bye Birdie* by Strouse and Adams	7 – 8
March of the Three Kings from *Amahl and the Night Visitors* by Gian-Carlo Menotti	1 – 6
Children's Symphony, First Movement by Harl McDonald	2 – 8
Merry Mount Suite by Howard Hanson	4 – 8
Humor from the *Afro-American Symphony* by William Grant Still	6 – 8
Chester from *New England Tryptych* by William Schuman	4 – 8
Father of Waters from *The Mississippi Suite* by Ferde Grofé	4 – 6
Variations on America by Charles Ives	1 – 8
American Salute by Morton Gould	1 – 8
Dream March and Circus Music from *The Red Pony* by Aaron Copland	1 – 4
Acadian Songs and Dances from *Louisiana Story* by Virgil Thompson	4 – 8
Walking Song and The Squeeze Box from Acadian Songs and Dances	1 –3
Allegro from Trio in A Minor, Op. 150 by Amy Beach	1 – 3 4 – 8
Suite for Wind Quintet by Ruth Crawford Seeger	6 – 8
A Piece for Tape Recorder by Vladimir Ussachevsky	6 – 8
Composition for Synthesizer by Milton Babbitt	6 – 8
Aria with Fontana Mix by John Cage	6 – 8

Lesson Title	Grades
Part Four: Moving with American Music	
Sally Go Round	K – 1
Pop! Goes the Weasel	K – 1
Toodala	K – 2
Hey Betty Martin	K – 2
One Day One Foot Kept Moving	K – 2
Bluebird	K – 2
All the Pretty Little Horses	K – 3
Chicken Reel	K – 2
	3 – 8
The Moccasin Song	K – 6
	K – 2
	3 – 6
Navajo Happy Song	2 – 3
The Syncopated Clock by Leroy Anderson	1 – 4
On the Fourth of July	2 – 5
Goodbye Old Paint	2 – 3
Love Somebody	K – 2
	3 – 6
Old Brass Wagon	K – 2
	3 – 8
Sourwood Mountain	4 – 8
Rounds for Dancing	4 – 8
The Sidewalks of New York	5 – 8
Stars and Stripes Forever by John Philip Sousa	K – 3
	4 – 8
Simple Gifts	4 – 8

21

Focus	Page

PART ONE

Singing American Music

SONGS OF EARLY AMERICA

President's March
Chester
Ballad Opera
Flora: or Hob in the Well
Old Hundredth
Shape Notes: Singing Schools

HUMOR IN MUSIC

Arkansas Traveler
Ain't Gonna Rain
Bought Me a Cat
I Wish I Was a Little Bird

COWBOYS

Red River Valley
Old Texas

THE GOLD RUSH

Camptown Races
Sacramento
We Are All Panning

FOR THE YOUNG

Mary Wore a Red Dress
Old Woman and Her Pig
Sweet Potato
Who's That?

CONTRAST AND VARIETY

Aloha
I'm Gonna Sing
Indian Melody
Rock Island Line
The Sidewalks of New York
Summertime
Wildwood Flower

SONGS PEOPLE BROUGHT WITH THEM

A Morning Song
Cherry Bloom
Lovely New Year Flower
Alouette

PATRIOTIC SONGS

Alaska's Flag
God Bless America
The Stars and Stripes Forever

Songs of Early America

THE PRESIDENT'S MARCH
(HAIL COLUMBIA)

Grades: 4 – 8

Focus: Performing historically important music.

Materials: (Optional) Recordings: Patriotic Songs of America, RCA WE91; Organ in America, Columbia ML 5496; Songs of the Presidency, Bowmar 598.

Procedure:

Philip Phile, a Philadelphian who came to this country from Germany, composed "The President's March" for the inauguration of George Washington. Later, when the words were written, the song became known as "Hail Columbia." It was the national anthem for about fifteen years.

- Present the words as a poem.
- Discuss the history of the song.
- Learn the chorus.
- Listen to the "President's March."

Enrichment:

- Learn the entire song.
- Lead research into the inauguration of George Washington.

Related activities:

- Present the film strip *Our Heritage of American Patriotic Songs* (Society for Visual Education Inc. No. 663.1, 2).
- Listen to other patriotic songs.
- Sing along with recordings of patriotic songs.

Hail Columbia

Joseph Hopkinson (words) 1798
Philip Phile (music) 1789

Grand Chorus

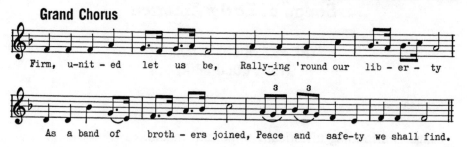

Firm, u–nit–ed let us be, Rally-ing 'round our lib–er–ty
As a band of broth–ers joined, Peace and safe-ty we shall find.

Verse

Hail Columbia, Happy land!
Hail ye heroes! heav'n born band!
Who fought and bled in freedom's cause,
Who fought and bled in freedom's cause.

CHESTER

by
William Billings

Grades: 5 – 6

Focus: Music of Early America – Revolutionary times.

Materials: None.

Procedure:

In 1770, William Billings, a Boston musician, produced *The New England Psalm Singer,* made up of 126 compositions in 4 and 5 parts. These were primarily psalms and hymn tunes with a few anthems and canons. The best known hymn is "Chester." Eight years later, Billings wrote four more stanzas, this time with anti-British words. This song became the best known song of the Revolutionary War.

- Say the words in rhythm like a marching song.
- Observe the slurs (more than one tone sung on one syllable).
- Sing the song with steady rhythm.

Enrichment:

Compose another verse about the Revolutionary War.

Chester

William Billings

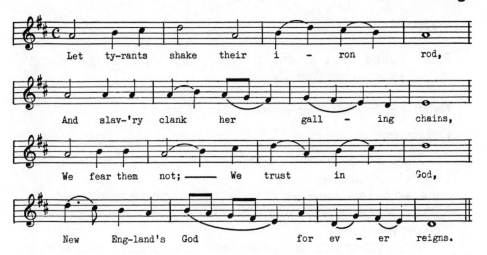

Let ty-rants shake their i - ron rod,

And slav-'ry clank her gall - ing chains,

We fear them not; —— We trust in God,

New Eng-land's God for ev - er reigns.

BALLAD OPERA

A ballad opera is a comic musical play. It consists of spoken dialogue interspersed with musical numbers, generally folk songs and dances popular at the moment. The transplanted songs are adapted to the plot of the opera. The use of borrowed songs is one of the great differences between ballad opera and the later musical comedy like *Oklahoma* where the music is specifically written for the play. Informal ballad opera might change at every performance. In early America, performances were advertised by the number of "airs" used.

Ballad opera was very popular in eighteenth century England. *The Beggar's Opera* by John Gay (1782) was the most popular English ballad opera. As the American colonists became established, they too had time for the arts, especially in communities like Newport, Boston, and Charleston. Ballad opera was a part of the social and cultural life in America until about the middle of the nineteenth century.

FLORA: or HOB IN THE WELL

A Ballad Opera
by
John Hippisley

Grades: 4 – 7

Focus: Ballad opera as entertainment; Comedy in song ("Young Hob's in the Well").

Materials: Optional – Improvised props, if staged.

Procedure:

Flora: or Hob in the Well, the first musical play in America, is a blend of comedy and romance. The story is about Flora, a young orphaned heiress, her lover, Friendly, and her severe guardian uncle, Sir Thomas Testy, who locks her in her room to prevent her from meeting young men.

When young Hob, the go-between, attempts to deliver a love letter to Flora from Friendly, arranging their elopement, he is caught by Sir Thomas and is thrown into the village well. Hob's rescue by his parents provides the comedy of the opera as he is alternately brought almost up, then dropped. In the end, Hob becomes a hero, Sir Thomas is thwarted, and the young lovers are married.

> Air IX (sung by Mr. Bates, a townsman)
>
> I never till now was conzarned in Strife
> Have Marcy, Sir Thomas, and spare poor Hob's Life.
> And give me my Freedom, as I had bevore –
> I'll be a good boy and I'll do zo no more.
>
> Indeed I won't – Sir. (Hob)

- Tell the story.
- Read the words of the song (The village bell calls the townspeople.) "Whoops! Down he goes again." etc.

- Learn the song.
- Repeat the song as many times as you want Hob to fall back into the well.
- Optional—Complete the story and dramatize.

Enrichment:

By changing the words, add familiar folk or currently popular tunes to the dramatization.

Young Hob's In The Well

based on an English folk tune from *Wit and Mirth of Pills to Purge Melancholy* edited by Thomas D'Urfey

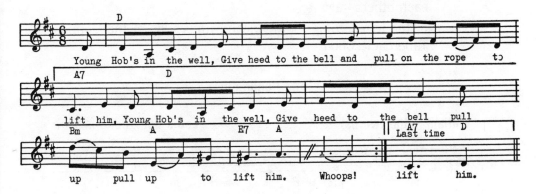

OLD HUNDREDTH

Grades: 4 – 8

Focus: Lining Out; Bay Psalm Book; Hymn Style.

Materials: "Old Hundredth."

Procedure:

When the Pilgrims came to the New World, they brought their Psalter containing the Psalms they had sung in England. Everyone knew the tunes. But gradually the old tunes were forgotten and singing in church was done by "lining out." A leader read or sang the words one line at a time and the congregation echoed their leader. Later, in some of the first academies, the monitor system was used. One student learned the song, then "lined it out" for the others.

The melody of "Old Hundredth" is attributed to Louis Bourgeois, editor of Calvin's *Genevan Psalter* published in 1551. The English Puritans used the same melody for their version of Psalm 100 in the 1640 *Bay Psalm Book,* said to be the first book printed in the Colonies.

- Line out "Old Hundredth." Notice the holds at the end of each line.
- Give at least two students the opportunity to be leader.
- Line out a new song planned for the next music session.

Enrichment:

- Encourage students to line out current songs, thus sharing each others' favorites.
- Listen to recordings of American hymns sung by the Mormon Tabernacle Choir.

Old Hundredth

William Kethe (words)   **Louis Bourgeois (music)**

SHAPE NOTES AND SINGING SCHOOLS

Grades: 4 – 8

Focus: Shape Notes; Reading music.

Materials: "Old Hundredth."

Procedure:

In 1710 the first singing school was formed to improve church singing and to teach the rudiments of music. As the number of schools grew, secular music was added to the hymns and psalms. Singing schools became a popular place for young people to meet each other. The schools spread through the colonies and west to Kentucky. Teachers often traveled from one settlement to another on horseback, charging small fees and holding evening meetings for a few weeks. Students generally furnished their own candles and contributed firewood.

The first books contained hymn tunes in three or four parts. The words were printed separately. William Billings of Boston was the most famous singing school teacher. To make the reading of music easier, shape notes (triangles, rectangles, diamonds, and ovals) were used. There were several systems designed by different teachers.

The singing school pointed up the spiritual, cultural and social values of music and laid the foundation for the teaching of music in public schools. In 1838, for the first time, the Boston schools required music to be taught.

This phrase of "Old Hundredth" is from the earliest known shape note book, *The Easy Instructor*, compiled in 1798 by William Little and William Smith, Philadelphia edition. The melody part was written in the tenor voice of a four-part score.

Old Hundredth

Sharp Key on A

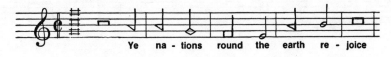

Ye   na - tions   round   the   earth   re - joice

Humor in Music

ARKANSAS TRAVELER

Grades: 4 – 8

Focus: Ballad singing; Instrumental accompaniment.

Materials: Chording instrument, melody instrument; Fiddle, banjo, keyboard, recorder.

Procedure:

The verses tell the story of the fiddler who couldn't remember the end of his tune and how a stranger finished it for him.

- Sing through the five verses to complete the story.
- Play the second part of the song on any available melody instrument.
- Make the score available to children who play an instrument, especially violin.
- Sketch the plan of the verses so that at the next lesson, students may completely memorize the words.

Away down south in Arkansas
The rain was wet, the wind was raw,
An old man sat on his porch that day
Atuning up his fiddle, then he started in to play.

Along came a stranger to his door;
Said he, "Old man, don't fiddle any more,
I'm cold and wet, I've walked all day
I'm looking for a fire and a place where I can stay."

The old man sat and fiddled his tune;
Said he, "I'm here to spend the afternoon.

You'd better travel down the road, my friend,
I know this tune's beginning, but I can't recall the end."

The stranger took a chair and sat right down;
"Look here," said he, "I've really been around.
I play a fiddle too, my fine old friend,
I know that tune's beginning and I know how it can end."

The old man smiled and winked his eye.
"That's great," said he, "I'm glad you happened by,
If you will only end this tune for me,
I'll set you by the fire and I'll brew a pot of tea."

Part Two

It's really very easy, for it travels right along,
Just fiddle away, you can hardly get it wrong,
I've been traveling through Arkansas everywhere they say,
There's not a better tune in all America today.

AIN'T GONNA RAIN

Grades: 2 – 6

Focus: Making up nonsense rhymes and singing them.

Materials: Rhythm or chop sticks (or use finger tips on table).

Procedure:

This nineteenth century ditty was popular in the East and South and came West with the settlers.

- Measures 1 and 2 and 5 and 6 are for making up nonsense words—the more outlandish, the better. Sometimes they form a question.
- Use the sticks to keep time and make a raindrop accompaniment.

- Other verses:

> Oh, what did the apple say to the worm,
> Go your way and leave me alone,
>
> The buttermilk's sour and the butter won't set
> Swing the partner you have met
>
> Cornbread's good and bacon's fat
> Give me bread and give me fat

- Original nonsense phrases may be sung individually with the class joining in on the alternate phrases.

BOUGHT ME A CAT

Cumulative Song

Grades: K – 4

Focus: Strong duple rhythm; Challenge of adding the verses.

Materials: (optional) Animal pictures made by the children; guitar.

Procedure:

- Sing the first verse until the children know the rhythm.
- Add clapping to the words.
- Add the second verse.
- Choose other animals to sing about.
- Decide on sounds for each.
- Add them in new verses. End each verse by singing all the preceding sounds in reverse order.

- If children have made animal pictures, they may stand when the appropriate sounds are sung.

Enrichment:

- Children may dramatize the song, singing the sounds and acting like the animals. (This may be done by solosits.)
- Children may choose and play rhythm instruments to accompany each animal sound.
- Form a parade of animals with each child making the sounds of previously chosen animals.

Related Activities

- Language arts. Make a list of animals (and birds), trying to make sounds of each.
- Develop this list into a story with music.

Bought Me a Cat

Traditional

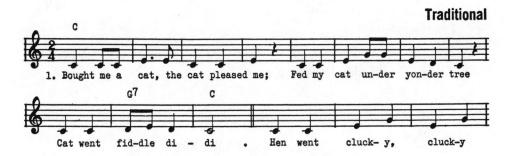

1. Bought me a cat, the cat pleased me; Fed my cat un-der yon-der tree
Cat went fid-dle di – di. Hen went cluck- y, cluck-y

2. Bought me a hen, the hen pleased me;
   Fed my hen under yonder tree
   Hen went clucky, clucky; Cat went fiddle di di.

3. Duck went quack, quack.
4. Cow went moo, moo.
5. Horse went neigh, neigh,
6. Sheep went baa, baa.
7. Pig went oink, oink.

After each added verse, sing all preceding sounds in reverse order, ending with "Cat went fiddle di di."

I WISH I WAS A LITTLE BIRD

Grades: K – 4

Focus: Solo singing and chanting; Humor in music.

Materials: none.

Procedure:

This old song was popular on outings such as picnics, boat rides, and other social gatherings of young people. The last phrase is really saying, "I want to be a part of the group."

- "Let's see if we can cheer up this lonesome singer."
- Sing the first three phrases. Speak the last one. Use an exaggerated, sorrowful voice. Pretend to cry.
- After the class knows the song, add the verse below.

      We all are little birds;
      We'll fly up in the tree.
      We'll sit and sing our happy little song.
      (Child's name optional), You don't have to stay by yourself!

                                                    (M.V.)

Enrichment:

Use other verses such as "fish . . . I'll swim down in a pool," "bear . . . I'll hide back in a cave."

I Wish I Was a Little Bird

Cowboys

RED RIVER VALLEY

Grades: 3 – 7

Focus: The spirit and importance of the cowboy song; Singing improvised verses.

Materials: Guitar or autoharp.

Procedure:

The Red River, the southernmost tributary of the Mississippi, runs through hundreds of miles of rich cattle land. The song "In the Bright Mohawk Valley," source of "Red River Valley," moved west with the cowboys and was adapted to the locale. On the long monotonous drives across the prairie to market points, the cowboys sang songs with countless improvised verses — many about love.

Red River Valley

Cowboy Song

2. Won't you think of the valley you're leaving?
   Oh, how lonely and sad it will be;
   Oh, think of the fond heart you're breaking
   And the grief you are causing to me.

Singing helped them forget how tired they were and also quieted the cattle.

Notice that the chorus repeats the melody of the verse and that the chord progression is the common I IV I V$_7$ I cadence.

- Sing the first verse and chorus at a comfortable tempo, like the slow gait of a cowboy's pony.
- Review the words. Discuss the cowboy's nomadic life style.
- Sing the song again with chordal accompaniment.
- Introduce the second verse, emphasizing the four line rhyming structure and the rhythm of the words.
- Suggest individual work on improvised verses.

OLD TEXAS

Grades: 4 – 8

Focus: Spirit of a cowboy song; Singing an echo song or modified round.

Materials: Chording instrument, wood block.

Procedure:

This song was popular when farmers were beginning to take over the grazing land in the Oklahoma territory. After Texas became a state in 1845, cattlemen began to look even further west for grazing land. The romantic life of the early cowboy was beginning to change.

The melody is made up primarily of chord tones—F A C and C E G. To make the parts harmonize, one tone in the second part—on the word "got"—is different. Otherwise, the two parts are exactly the same.

- Sing Part One as a unison song until it is familiar. Keep strict time.
- Add a chording instrument.
- Sing Part Two as a unison song. Point out the one different note.
- Add a chording instrument.
- Divide the class into two sections.
- Sing the parts together.

- Add a wood block accompaniment on the third verse (short long, short long).
- Students change parts and repeat the song.

Old Texas

Oklahoma Cowboy Song

The Gold Rush

Camptown Races
(Sacramento)

by
Stephen Foster

Grades: 4 – 6

Focus: Stephen Foster; Arranging a song to fit the occasion.

Materials: (Optional) banjo, guitar, autoharp; Music score.

Procedure:

Stephen Foster wrote 189 songs. Most of these were of two very different kinds—lively minstrel and nonsense songs and romantic ballads. "Camptown Races" (as well as "Oh! Susanna") was written about the time of the California Gold Rush. Many ships sailed around the Cape of South America and up the West Coast to San Francisco. Sailors brought Foster's popular song along with them and changed it to suit the occasion.

Camptown Races

- Sing the song with spirit.
- Use hands and feet to keep time as you sing it again.
- Sing it with part of the students answering with the "Doodahs."
- Experiment with clapping patterns—on the "Doodahs," on the refrain, on the rhythm of the words.

Sacramento

- Sing the song carefully, noting the differences from "Camptown Races."

- Add another verse about the Gold Rush.
- Add banjo, guitar or autoharp.

Enrichment:

Sing "Oh! Susanna," the favorite song on the wagon trails to California.

Camptown Races

The Camptown ladies sing this song, Doodah! Doodah!
The Camptown race track five miles long, Oh Doodah day!

Chorus:
Goin' to run all night! Goin' to run all day!
I'll bet my money on the bobtail nag.
Somebody bet on the bay.

2. I came down there with my hat caved in, Doodah! Doodah!
   I go back now with a pocketful of tin, Oh day! Doodah!

Sacramento

As I was walking on the quay, Hoodah, to my hoodah,
A pretty girl I chanced to see, Hoodah, hoodah day.

Chorus:
Blow boys blow for California.
There's plenty of gold so I've been told.
On the banks of the Sacramento.

WE ARE ALL PANNING

by
Mark Taylor

Grades: 3 – 7

Focus: Entertainment in the Gold Rush Years; Singing about events of the day.

Materials: Background material about the California Gold Rush.

Procedure:

Mark Taylor was an itinerant entertainer and singer who traveled from one mining town to another, encouraging the miners in their frenzied attempts to find a golden fortune. In each town he manufactured songs, always praising the miners and lampooning the life and politics of the times. In other verses of this song he disparages the preacher, the politicians, and attorneys, then exposes them as rascals all.

This song is taken from *"The Gold Digger's Song Book* containing the most popular humorous and sentimental songs composed by M. Taylor and sung by his original company with unbounded applause throughout California."

- Discuss the Gold Rush and the hardships of the forty-niners, the building of the mining towns, and the panning of gold.
- Read the song in rhythm.
- Sing the first verse. (This may be a chorus between each verse.)
- After the first verse is quite familiar to all, add other verses.

Enrichment:

Dramatize the song and include it in a culminating activity about the gold rush.

Related Activities:

Sing "Oh! Susanna" and "Sacramento."

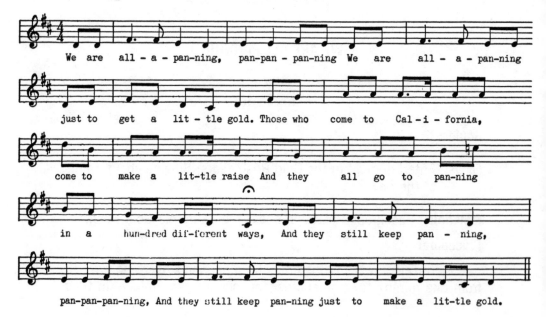

The Gold Digger's Song Book by Mark Taylor, Marysville Daily Herald Print 1856, reprinted in a limited edition by the Book Club of California, 1975. Used by permission.

For the Young

MARY WORE A RED DRESS

Grades: K – 1

Focus: Using music to teach colors and objects of clothing.

Materials: None.

Procedure:

- Sing this five-tone song as written.
- Discuss the color red. Point out something red.
- Sing the song using the name of the child wearing red.
- Repeat the song using different colors, pointing out as many children as possible.

Enrichment:

Use this melody and idea to develop other basic concepts of size, sound, temperature, etc.

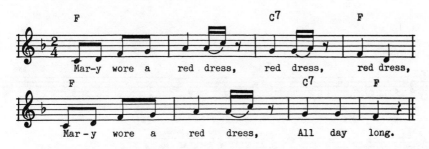

THE OLD WOMAN AND HER PIG

Grades: K – 2

Focus: Introducing ballad style music; Answering back phrases; How to hum.

Materials: (optional) C and D bells; Chording instrument.

Procedure:

Pseudo-sad songs have always been popular with children. They understand the tongue-in-cheek humor. "Old woman" songs and stories are a recognized part of American literature for children.

Some stories have a moral to tell; others, like this one, are just for fun.

- Introduce the humming "Mmm-Mmm-mm." Challenge each child to hum mysteriously, in mock sorrow, or as if to say, "Isn't that too bad?" Accompany with the C and D bells.
- Sing the song as a story, including the children in the humming responses.
- Repeat the song with the children singing along.

Enrichment:

Vary the song by singing the response "Oink, oink, oink."

Related Activities:

Tell other "old lady" stories.

The Old Woman and Her Pig

Traditional

2. Now, this old woman kept the pig in the barn,
   Prettiest little thing she had on the farm.

3. Oh, that little pig did a heap of harm,
   He made tracks all around the barn.

4. Now, this old woman fed the pig on clover,
   It lay down and died all over.

5. Now, this old tale's from the book on the shelf,
   If you want any more you can sing it yourself.

SWEET POTATO

Grades: K – 2

Focus: Strong syncopated rhythm in song; Expressing words and rhythms with movement.

Materials: (Optional) small drum, maracas.

Procedure:

This song is a children's version of the bamboula dance. The strong rhythm makes you want to move as you sing.

- Sing the song, exaggerating the accent on count one.
- Sing the song again, tapping strongly with the *left* foot on count one and the *right* foot on the off beat.
- Challenging: Sing again and *add* clapping or slapping thighs to the foot rhythms.
- Not so challenging: Divide the rhythms between two groups.
- Sing and move around the room in a line.
- Sing, move, and clap. If drums or maracas are available, add them. Play the drum on count one, the maracas on off beats.

Traditional

Sweet po-ta - to, Hot sweet po-ta - to, Sweet po-ta- to, Sweet po-ta-to; Hot!

Enrichment:

Listen to *Bamboula* by Gottschalk.

WHO'S THAT?

Grades: K – 1

Lesson One

Focus: Individual – Group dramatization; Distinguishing between tapping and knocking.

Materials: Window – door.

Procedure:

- Sing the song, demonstrating tapping and knocking.
- Children sing and demonstrate on the table.
- Choose one child to *tap* on the *window,* then *knock* on the *door.*
- Child dramatizes. Group sings. Use name of child. Take turns.

Lesson Two

Focus: Adapting words to action; Building vocabulary.

- Sing the song using "walking by my window," "stopping at my door."
- One child dramatizes.
- Other children dramatize in turn.
- Change words to "tapping on my wall," "knocking on my table."
- Continue dramatization using actions in different order.
- Use similar phrases until all objects in the room are identified. (tap chair, knock floor, tap desk, knock toy box)

Who's that tap-ping at my win – dow? Who's that knock-ing at my door?
(name   ) tap-ping at my win – dow? (name   ) knock-ing at my door?

Contrast and Variety

ALOHA OE

Grades: 3 – 8

Focus: Singing with good tone quality and accurate enunciation; Basic ukulele strums.

Materials: One or more ukulele(s).

Procedure:

This song was written by the last reigning Hawaiian Island queen, Liliuokalani. It has become a popular song of farewell, especially when leaving the islands.

- Learn the chorus first. Sing on the vowels and sound every consonant.
- Learn the C chord; the G chord; The D_7 chord.
- Practice moving from C to G to D_7 to G to C to D_7 to G
- Strum even quarter notes on G G C G/G G D_7 D_7/G G G as an introduction.
- Sing the chorus with ukulele accompaniment.
- Introduce the verse as a four line stanza. (Memorize it at the next lesson.)

Enrichment:

- Elaborate on the basic strum.
- Encourage solo singing.

Aloha Oe
Farewell to Thee

        G   C   G
Proudly glides the rain cloud o'er the cliffs,

      D_7
Blown onward by the gentle breeze;

        G   C   G
How the scene recalls the distant past,

      C D_7 G
And I live once again my memories.

Chorus:

      C   G
Farewell to thee, farewell to thee,

      D$_7$ G
O beauteous one who lives among the flowers,

      C   G
One fond embrace before I leave

     D$_7$ G
Until we meet again.

I'M GONNA SING

Grades: 1 – 8

Focus: Joy of singing.

Materials: None.

Procedure:

This spiritual is a religious song of the black American culture. It seems to be a coupling of African music and the nineteenth century revivalist gospel song. All spirituals imply religious fervor. Some have rather complex rhythms.

After the Civil War, traveling choruses from Fisk University and Tuskegee Institute and other schools made the spiritual famous all over the United States. In the twentieth century, the spiritual, like the blues, has become a growing part of the popular music idiom.

This is a happy spiritual and lends itself to body rhythms as accompaniment. Other verses are "shout," "preach," "pray."

- Sing the song in strict rhythm.
- Sing it again, accenting counts one and three with foot tapping or head movements.
- Sing it again and clap the off beats two and four.
- Sing other verses, the ones above or verses of motion like "I'm gonna walk, rock, tap, etc."

Enrichment:

- Harmonize by ear.
- Elaborate on the rhythm and/or melody.

I'm Gonna Sing

Spiritual

I'm gon-na sing when the spir-it says, "Sing," I'm gon-na sing when the spir-it says,

"Sing," I'm gon-na sing when the spir-it says, "Sing," And o - bey the spir-it of the Lord.

INDIAN MELODY

Lesson One

Grades: 1 – 4

Focus: Melody without words.

Materials: Finger drum.

Procedure:

This calm melody from the Indians of the Lake Superior region is like a lullaby. Singing it with a neutral syllable or a word without specific meaning is appropriate. Use "way, loo, woo, whoo," or humming.

- Sing the melody with "way."
- Sing it again and keep time with the fingers on a small drum.
- Hum the tune.
- Children may talk about what the melody means to them.
- Sing the melody once more.

Lesson Two

Focus: Playing the bells by ear, using fragments of the melody.

Materials: Resonator bells C D F G A, or any mallet bells. (You may designate the bells to be used by attaching bits of colored tape.)

- Teacher plays the first phrase on the bells.
- Children sing with the bells.
- Teacher plays the second phrase.
- Children sing with the bells.
- Teacher plays the third phrase.
- Children sing with the bells.

Extension of Lesson Two:

- Ask for a volunteer to play a short original phrase on the bells.
- Children sing the melody with this original background.
- Give several children an opportunity to play the bells.
- Leave the bells available for individual exploration. This exploration will be the basis for the next lesson—making up original melodies.

Indian Melody
Chippewa Song

THE ROCK ISLAND LINE

Grades: 3 – 6

Focus: Singing an American work song; Keeping a regular syncopated beat and developing a vocal ostinato (short repeated accompaniment pattern).

Materials: Keyboard.

Procedure:

The Rock Island Line built the first bridge across the Mississippi River.

- Sing the song softly but with a strong accent.
- Sing again, tapping feet on the strong beats (1 and 3).
- Repeat, adding clapping on the off beats (2 and 4).
- Sing the fragment "Rock Island Line."
- Sing the song again with three or four people repeating the fragment as an accompaniment.
- Teacher or a student plays the keyboard rhythm.
- Combine singing, clapping, tapping, vocal ostinato, and keyboard rhythms.

Enrichment:

Add sandblocks or shakers playing a chug-chug-chug-chug accompaniment.

The Rock Island Line

Traditional Work Song

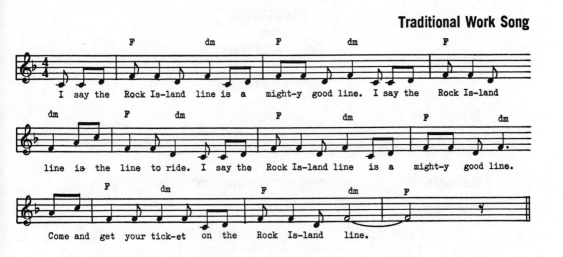

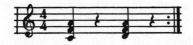

THE SIDEWALKS OF NEW YORK

(Refrain)

Grades: 4 – 8

Focus: Harmonizing by ear.

Materials: (Optional) chording instrument.

Procedure:

- Sing the melody. (The music is in Part Four, *Patterned Movement.*)
- While some continue to sing the melody, others try harmonizing. Start singing a third below the melody. This will sound good most of the time. When it does not, experiment with other tones or sing in unison.
- If a chording instrument is used, listen to it. You will get your cue from the chords.
- Encourage students to try harmonizing outside of class.

SUMMERTIME
from
Porgy and Bess
by
George Gershwin

Grades: 6 – 8

Focus: Rhythmic singing of the lullaby "Summertime."

Materials: Score or recording of "Summertime."

Procedure:

Porgy and Bess is a black folk opera in the blues idiom. The setting is Catfish Row, a tenement community. It is the love story of Porgy a crippled beggar who gets around in his goat cart, and his woman, Bess. Crown, the huge stevedore who murders a man and then escapes, and Sporting Life, the dope peddler who constantly tempts Bess, complicate the action. Clara and others in the community are the supporting characters. The action, which includes a killer hurricane, is fast and violent. When Crown returns for Bess, Porgy strangles him. While Porgy is in jail, Sporting Life takes Bess with him to New York. The opera ends with Porgy driving off to New York to find Bess.

In the first scene, in the court yard, Clara sings "Summertime" as she sits with her baby in her arms, rocking it back and forth. The song comforts the baby with "nothin' can harm you."

Bess sings the first verse again in the second act as she cares for Clara's baby.

Other famous songs from the opera are "I Got Plenty of Nothin'," and "It Ain't Necessarily So."

- Give a brief resumé of the story.
- Identify the song's place in the opera.
- Sing the song with a recording or piano accompaniment.
- Start memorization of the song. (Check progress next lesson.)

Enrichment:

- Sing or listen to other songs from the opera.
- Listen to the entire opera.

WILDWOOD FLOWER

Grades: 6 – 8

Focus: The Carter family; Singing in country music style with dulcimer, guitar, or autoharp.

Materials: Chordal instrument.

Procedure:

The Carter family made this song famous in their early hillbilly and country music programs. The romantic words reflect the rural setting of nineteenth and early twentieth century Appalachia. The melody may be noted on the dulcimer using the Ionian tuning C G G and starting on the fifth fret. The open string "bum biddy bum" drone accompaniment will sound somewhat like a bagpipe. An accompaniment on the guitar may be as simple or as elaborate as the guitarist is able to make it.

- Learn the song. Sing in a relaxed manner. Breathe between prepositional phrases.
- Guitarist or autoharp player practices the chords.
- Sing song with the instrument.
- A dulcimer player will need time to practice alone before noting the melody as an accompaniment.

Enrichment:

Develop a country music program. Elaborate on the melody.

Related Activities:

Listen to recordings of the Carter family.

Wildwood Flower

Appalachian Song

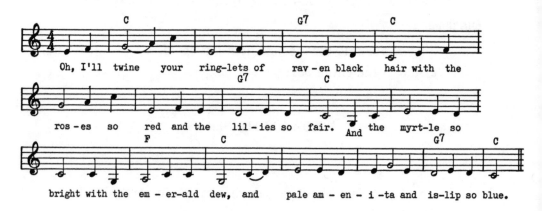

Oh, I'll twine your ring-lets of rav-en black hair with the ros-es so red and the lil-ies so fair. And the myrt-le so bright with the em-er-ald dew, and pale am-en-i-ta and is-lip so blue.

Songs People Brought With Them

A MORNING SONG
Las Mañanitas

Grades: 4 – 6

Focus: Harmonizing in thirds; Singing a serenade from Mexico.

A Morning Song
(Las Mañanitas)

Translated by Olcutt and Phyllis Sanders
Based on English text by Janet E. Tobitt

Mexican Folk Song

To use as a birthday song, change the last two lines of the verse to:

And since here it is your birthday,   *Por ser dia de tu santo*
For you this music we bring.   *Te las cantamos a ti.*

Alternate verse:

Happy birthday dear (. . .), a happy birthday to you we sing!
As of old a morning greeting was sung by David the King.

Materials: Keyboard and/or guitar.

Procedure:

"Las Mañanitas" is used not only as a birthday greeting but also as a morning or evening serenade.

Harmonizing in thirds is the easiest and the most natural kind of harmonizing.

- Choose the verse appropriate for the group.
- Sing the verse.
- Repeat the words several times.
- Sing the chorus.
- Repeat the words several times.
- Sing the entire song.
- Repeat the chorus. The teacher leads one group in harmonizing. The keyboard may be used the first time, only.
- Use the guitar anytime during the lesson.

Enrichment:

Sing the song in Spanish.

CHERRY BLOOM
(Sakura)

Grades: 4 – 8

Focus: Singing a Japanese song; minor pentatonic scale.

Materials: Guitar, violin, autoharp, or other stringed instrument.

Procedure:

Cherry blossoms symbolize spring and beauty. As a symbol of friendship, the Japanese government presented the grove of cherry trees planted in Washington D.C. around the tidal basin.

The song is sometimes played on the koto, a Japanese instrument with thirteen strings. The player sits on the floor and plucks the strings. Plucking the strings on any available instrument adds an Oriental flavor to the song.

The song is constructed on 1, 2, 3, 5, 6 of the minor scale. This could be called the minor pentatonic scale or five note scale.

It will probably take more than one lesson for this song to become very familiar.

- Sing or play the entire song.
- Sing the first phrase (measures 1 – 4);
- Then the second phrase (measures 4 – 8);
- Then the third phrase.
- Note that the third phrase starts like the second phrase but has a different ending.
- Sing the last two measures. This is a kind of invitation to cherry blossom time.
- Sing the entire song. One student may pluck the melody (or the first note in each measure) to help the singing.

Extension of the lesson:

- Make available the five bells (resonator) of the song.

- Exploration of the scale, finding phrases of the song, and creating original melodies—all increase the understanding of this kind of music.

Enrichment:

Sing the Japanese words.

> Sakura Sakura Yayoino sora wa
> Miwatasu kagiri Kasumi ka kumoka
> Nioi zo izuru.
> Sakura Sakura ah, Sakura.

Cherry Bloom
Sakura

Japanese Folk Song

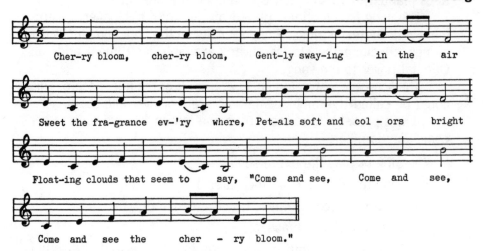

Cher-ry bloom,   cher-ry bloom,   Gent-ly sway-ing   in the   air

Sweet the fra-grance ev-'ry   where,   Pet-als soft and   col - ors   bright

Float-ing clouds that seem to   say,   "Come and see,   Come and   see,

Come   and   see   the   cher - ry   bloom."

LOVELY NEW YEAR FLOWER

Grades: 3 – 8

Focus: Major pentatonic scale.

Materials: Recorder or flute (optional).

Procedure:

The traditional New Year's flower, the narcissus (called Sui Sin Fa), is a symbol of friendship and understanding. It is valued as a decoration for the Chinese New Year which is celebrated in January or February. Celebrations are held in San Francisco and other American cities where there is a large Chinese population.

This song contains 1, 2, 3, 5, 6 of the major scale—the major pentatonic scale. Note that the melody of the first phrase (measures 1–2) is repeated (measures 3–4). Since the song is quite different from the traditional American folk song, it may take more than one lesson to become very familiar with the melody.

- Using the syllable "la" sing phrases 1 and 2.
- Sing this with the words.

- Sing the rest of the song several times.
- Sing the entire song with the recorder or flute playing the melody. This helps the singing.

Extension of the lesson:

- Encourage students to play phrases of the song on the bells (low and high C, D, E, G, A)
- Any short original phrases created by students may be used as a background or ostinato with the song.

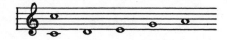

Lovely New Year Flower

Words by Madu Lee
Chinese Folk Song

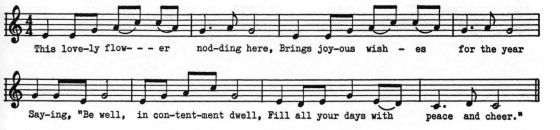

This love-ly flow- - - er nod-ding here, Brings joy-ous wish - es for the year

Say-ing, "Be well, in con-tent-ment dwell, Fill all your days with peace and cheer."

From *Growing with Music* by Harry R. Wilson, Walter Ehret, Alice M. Snyder, and Edward J. Hermann; Prentice-Hall Inc., Englewood Cliffs, N.J. 1963. Used by permission.

ALOUETTE

Grades: 3 – 8

Focus: Singing a cumulative song; Singing in French.

Materials: (Optional) French words on chart or chalk board.

Procedure:

- Sing the first line. Translate.
- Sing the rest of the verse. Translate.

- Repeat the verse until it is very familiar.
- Add verses. Sing all preceding additions in reverse order. End each verse with "Alouette, alouette" before each D.C.

  Order of verses: la tête (head) (tet); la bec (beak) (beck); le nez (nose) (nay); le dos (back) (doe); les pattes (claws) (paht); le cou (neck) (coo).

  Other pronunciations: (to pluck) (plue-meh-ray); gentille alouette (a gentle dove) (john-tee ah-loo-eh-teh); je te (which I) (je tuh).

Alouette

French Canadian Folk Song

Patriotic Songs

ALASKA'S FLAG

Grades: 4 – 8

Focus: Accurate articulation in singing; Description and meaning of the state flag.

Materials: (Optional) chordal accompaniment.

Procedure:

Benny Benson, son of an Aleut-Russian mother and a Swedish father, was thirteen years old when he entered his flag design in the American Legion contest. From a total of 142 designs, Benny's was chosen winner and was officially adopted as the state flag by the Alaska Territorial Legislature in 1927. The flag has the dipper constellation on the left and center and the North Star in the upper right. Here is Benny's explanation of his design:

"The blue field is for the Alaska sky and the forget-me-not, an Alaskan flower. The North Star is for the future state of Alaska, the most northerly of the union. The dipper is for the Great Bear — symbolizing strength." (Courtesy of the State of Alaska.)

Benny was awarded a cash scholarship and a gold watch. He used the scholarship to learn about diesel engines in a school in Seattle. The gold watch is now in the Alaska State Museum.

The words of the song were written by Marie Drake (1888–1963) who worked in the Alaskan Department of Education for twenty-eight years. The music was written by Elinor Dusenburg. It is the official state song of Alaska. The United States bought Alaska from Russia in 1867. It became the 49th state in 1959.

- Read the words of the song and discuss the meaning. Emphasize these things—the constellations, sourdough, the climate, the Aurora Borealis, statehood.
- Discuss the flag.
- Tell the story of Benny Benson.
- Learn the song phrase by phrase.

Enrichment:

Illustrate the song.

Related Activities:

- Research the state song and flag of the children's home state.
- Develop a banner for the class. Create a chant or song to go with the banner.

Alaska's Flag

Marie Drake   **Elinor Dusenbury**

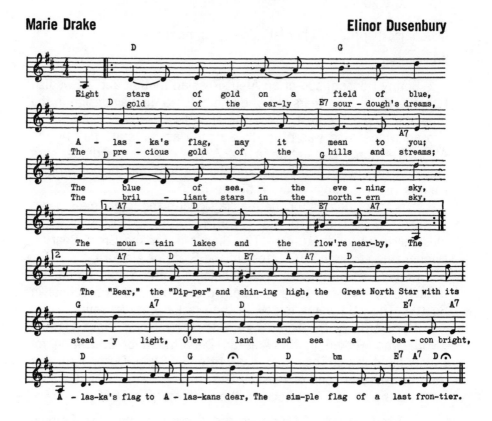

GOD BLESS AMERICA

by
Irving Berlin

Grades: 3 – 8

Focus: Singing with free voice and feeling.

Materials: Score of the song.

Procedure:

Irving Berlin progressed from singing waiter to song writer. Weaving words and music together, he wrote many popular songs that remain in the standard American repertoire. His lyrics were often about current happenings, bond drives during the war, politics and celebrities.

"God Bless America" was first performed by Kate Smith, popular radio singer, on Armistice Day (later Veterans Day) in 1938. It has become a national favorite. Many people like to think of it as the unofficial anthem. It is easy to sing and expresses love and concern for our country.

In 1954, Irving Berlin received a citation of merit from President Eisenhower for writing "God Bless America" and other patriotic songs. Berlin donated all royalties from the song to the Girl Scouts and Boy Scouts of America.

- Introduce the chorus in march time. Sing with a relaxed but firm accent.
- To help students memorize the chorus, divide the words into a four line stanza.
- Discuss the background of the composer and song.
- Sing the chorus from memory. Note weaknesses to be stressed in next lesson.

Enrichment:

Learn the verse, also as a four line stanza.

Related Activities:

Listen to songs from Berlin's musical comedy *Annie Get Your Gun,* the story of Annie Oakley from Buffalo Bill's Wild West Show.

THE STARS AND STRIPES FOREVER
Trio
Words and Music by John Philip Sousa

Grades: 4 – 8

Focus: Two-part singing (May also be sung in unison); Singing a patriotic song.

Materials: Score for Trio of "The Stars and Stripes Forever"; (Optional) accompaniment.

Procedure:

"The Stars and Stripes Forever" was written for band when John Philip Sousa was director of the United States Marine Band in Washington D.C. from 1880 to 1892. The words he wrote for the Trio of the band piece reflect the loyalty he had for his country.

This piece is harmonized mostly in thirds, the easiest interval for harmonizing.

- Present the words and the melody line (soprano), emphasizeing the beat and the pronunciation of the words.
- (Optional) Repeat the words as a chant to the rhythm of the melody.
- Sing the song again.
- Children sing with the keyboard playing the alto part.
- All sing the alto part as the keyboard plays both parts.
- Divide the class into two parts, each singing one part.
- Repeat, reversing the parts.

> Hurrah for the flag of the free,
> May it wave as our standard forever,
> The gem of the land and the sea,
> The banner of the right!
> Let tyrants remember the day
> When our fathers with mighty endeavor,
> Proclaimed as they marched to the fray,
> That by their might and by their right it waves forever.

Enrichment:

Stage this with a drill team of sixteen students marching and singing.

Related Activities:

Listen to "Semper Fideles" by Sousa.

PART TWO

Playing American Instruments

THE AUTOHARP

THE BANJO

MALLET BELLS

THE BUGLE

INDIAN DRUMS AND
OTHER INSTRUMENTS

DRUMS IN BANDS, ORCHESTRAS,
POPULAR GROUPS

   Parade Drums

THE APPALACHIAN DULCIMER

THE GUITAR

THE HARMONICA

KEYBOARDS

THE RECORDER

THE UKULELE

WHISTLING, WHISTLES, AND THE
FIFE

INFORMAL INSTRUMENTS

   Bones
   Jaw Harp
   Jug
   Kazoo
   Washtub Bass

Playing American Instruments

In this book, American instruments are defined as those that have been used extensively by Americans in United States history and/or are now being used by both professional and amateur musicians to play American music.

We think of some instruments as being exclusively American. But, since variations of blowing, scraping, and hitting music-making devices are universal, it may be impossible to say that any instruments are truly nationalistic, except in their adaptations. Even the Appalachian dulcimer and the banjo (the most American of instruments) have their roots in the Orient and Africa.

However, because of their utilitarian and, sometimes, affectionate and joyful use by Americans, certain instruments have effectively become American.

This section includes descriptions of these instruments, elementary playing instructions for them, American music to play on them, and, in some cases, a guide for making the instruments, themselves.

The Autoharp

The autoharp is a set of chromatically tuned strings stretched over the soundboard top of a wooden case. It is really a zither with push button chords. When a button is depressed, the chord bar mutes all strings except those used in the chord. For example, for the C major chord only the C, E, and G strings are left free to vibrate. For the G7 chord, only the G, B, D, and F strings are left free.

To play the autoharp, hold it on your lap, across your chest, or set it on a table. Push the chord buttons with the left fingers. With your right hand, strum away from you, using the back of your nails or a pick.

Table of Chords

Songs may be transposed up or down by using corresponding chords. Guitar, keyboard, or ukulele symbols may be used for the autoharp. (Note: Some models do not have all these chords.)

KEY	BASIC CHORDS (I, IV, V7)			ENRICHMENT CHORDS				
C	C,	F,	G7	D7,	A7,	E7,	a min,	d min
F	F,	Bb,	C7	G7,	D7,	A7,	d min,	g min
G	G,	C,	D7	A7,	E7,	a min		
D	D,	G,	A7	E7				
A	A,	D,	E7					
a min	a min,	d min,	E7					
d min	d min,	g min,	A7	E7				

PLAYING THE AUTOHARP

Grades: 3 – 8

Basic Focus: Establishing playing skills on the autoharp.

Materials: One or more autoharps.

Procedure:

- Familiarize yourself with the song.
- Establish the chord button pattern under your fingers.
- Whenever possible, keep the same fingers on the same buttons throughout.

- Practice moving quickly from one chord to another. (Follow the chord sequence of the song.) Memorize as much as possible.
- Using the chord-strum markings over the words as a guide, practice rhythmic strumming while making chord changes. (Strum on either side of the chord bar.)
- Use the chord-strum pattern for the last line of the song as an introduction or between-verse interlude.
- Play through at least once by yourself before accompanying singers.
- You're ready to accompany the singers.
- After the study of the basic strums you will be able to create your own variations.

Go Tell Aunt Rhody
```
4 G  G      G  G  D7        D7  G
4 Go tell aunt Rho-dy, Go tell aunt Rho-dy,
  G  G      G  G   D7      D7      G
  Go tell aunt Rho-dy, the old gray goose is dead.
```

(2) The one she was saving . . . To make a feather bed.
(3) She died in the mill pond . . . Standing on her head.
(4) The goslings are crying . . . Because the goose is dead.
(5) The gander is weeping . . . Because his mate is dead.

Jingle Bells
```
   F     F  F     F    F     F      F
Jin-gle bells, jin-gle bells, Jin-gle all the way,
Bb      F   F   F       G7        G7        C7
Oh, what fun it is to ride in a one-horse o-pen sleigh!
   F     F  F     F    F     F      F
Jin-gle bells, jin-gle bells, Jin-gle all the way,
Bb      F   F   F       C7        C7      F F
Oh, what fun it is to ride, in a one-horse o-pen sleigh!
```

Home on the Range
```
6    (F)G        G           (Bb)C     C
8 Oh, give me a home where the buf-fa-lo roam.
          (F)G        G7 A7    (C7)D7
  Where the deer and the an-te-lope play;
          (F)G        G   (Bb)C           C
  Where sel-dom is heard a dis-cour-ag-ing word,
          (F)G        (C7)D7    (F)G
  And the skies are not cloud-y all day.
```

(F)G   (G₇) D₇   (F)G
Home, home on the range,
              (F)G   (G₇)A₇   D₇
Where the deer and the an-te-lope play;
      (F)G   G   (B♭)C   C
Where sel-dom is heard a dis-cour-ag-ing word,
          (F)G   (C₇) D₇   (F)G
And the skies are not cloud-y all day.

The Banjo

The modern banjo is probably a descendent of a Western African instrument which was a kind of an open drum with a wooden neck and several strings stretched over it.

The five string banjo as we know it today was developed about the time Stephen Foster was writing songs. Today it is a popular jazz instrument and a happy sounding accompanying instrument for American folk songs.

THE BANJO

Lesson One

Grades: 4 – 8

Focus: Tuning, Holding, Strumming and Picking.

Materials: One or more banjos.

Procedure:

Tuning with a Piano

Tune each string to match the pitch of the corresponding piano key. Notice that the short string is tuned to a higher G. (The banjo may also be tuned to a banjo pitchpipe which is a set of small tubes tuned one octave higher than the open strings. Be sure to tune one octave lower than the pitchpipe.)

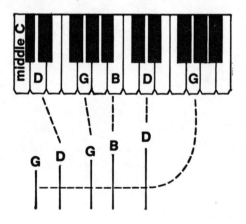

Holding

Hold the banjo in your lap pressed against your chest, your right forearm ready to strum over the parchment head. The neck will be at an angle.

Strumming and Picking

The thumb, index and middle fingers are used for both strumming and picking. With your right hand in a loose fist, flick the nail of your middle finger down across the strings. Try picking with your index finger. To alternate picking and strumming, pick up one string with the index finger, then strum down with your middle finger.

- Hold the banjo.
- Strum with the correct hand position and finger.
- Practice strumming.
- The chord produced from strumming the open strings is the G major chord. Strum as you sing or hum "Row, Row, Row Your Boat."
- Strum a bugle call as you sing it with "Tu, tu."

Enrichment:

Try picking and strumming the accompaniment for the same melodies.

Related Activities:

Learn the song "Ring, Ring the Banjo" by Stephen Foster.

Lesson Two

Focus: The D₇ Chord; Accompanying familiar songs.

Procedure:

D₇ Chord   1 = index finger
            2 = middle finger

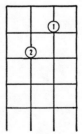

- Finger the D$_7$ chord.
- Strum the D$_7$ chord with your middle finger. Strum only the long strings.
- Alternate strumming the D$_7$ chord with picking the 5th string G with your index finger.
- Alternate strumming the open strings (G chord) and the D$_7$ chord.
- Strum to keep time for "Red River Valley" or "Old Brass Wagon."

Mallet Bells

Mallet bells have been in American classrooms for many years. Like a glockenspiel, they are rectangular steel plates arranged and tuned in the same order as a piano keyboard. Some are made of wood like a xylophone. They are played by striking the bars with mallets made of hard rubber or wood. The mallet is held firmly near the end and bounced on the center of the bell bar.

ESCALATOR SONG

Grades: K – 3

Focus: Developing playing techniques; Playing a scale song.

Materials: One or more sets of bells (attached or resonator).

Procedure:

- Bell players bounce the mallet(s) on low C.
- Bounce mallets on D, E, F, G, A, B, C.
- All sing the song. On the second singing the children may move up and down to establish the feeling of low to high and back.
- Bell players play, singing letter names (another verse).
- Bell players accompany the singing.

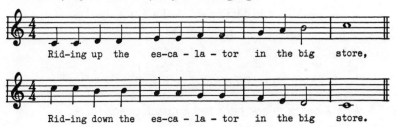

OLD McDONALD

Grades: K – 3

Focus: Hearing and re-creating a melody; Reinforcing the concept of melody (up, down, the same).

Materials: Resonator bells D♭, E♭, G♭, A♭, B♭; (On attached bells mark bars with tape).

Procedure:

Re-creating a melody without using notation is called playing by ear. Some children will be able to play all of "Old McDonald" while others may play one or two motifs. This lesson uses the song as already familiar to the children.

- Put the set of five bells on a table.
- Give the first clue. "Old McDonald" starts on G♭ (1). Does it go up or down?" (down to D♭). Then where does it go? (to E♭)."
- Sing "E-i, e-i, o." Find the bars for this much.
- Give the bell players time to explore and find the motifs.
- One child may play the G♭ bar for all the "Quacks."
- Find these bits of the song (Had a farm) (On this farm) (With a quack).
- Children sing the song while the bell players accompany them with any parts they have discovered.

Enrichment:

- Make the bells available for further improvision.
- Use other sets of bars to play the song in other keys. (C, D, F, G, A) (D, E, G, A, B) (A, B, D, E, F♯).

Old McDonald Had a Farm

```
    1        5  6    5   3   2  1
Old McDonald had a farm, E-I, E-I, O,
    1        5  6    5   3   2  1
On this farm he had a duck, E-I, E-I, O.
    5    1             5     1
With a quack quack here and a quack quack there,
    1
Here a quack, There a quack, Everywhere a quack, quack,
    1        5  6    5   3  2  1
Old McDonald had a farm, E-I, E-I, O.
```

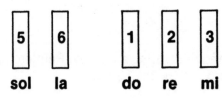

The Bugle

The Bugle and, later, the army field trumpet, have been used for communication signals in the armed forces since the Revolutionary War. Only five tones are needed for the many calls. Variety and interest are achieved by tempo, dynamics, and by the many rhythmic combinations in the calls. The calls may be played on any diatonic instrument such as recorder, keyboard or bells. They may also be sung through a kazoo.

Listening Materials
  1. *The Spirit of '76* (to the Civil War) Mercury MG50111
  2. *Music for Field Trumpets and Drums* Mercury MG 50112

BUGLE CALL

Grades: 1 – 8

Focus: C Major chord; Assembly Call.

Materials: A melodic instrument such as recorder, keyboard, or bells.

Procedure:

Assembly Call

- Play the C major chord – C E G.
- Play the G below the C.
- Play G C E G.
- Sing the rhythm of the call with "Tu."
- Play the call on the instrument. (See the lesson on the instrument used, for playing techniques.)

Indian Drums and Other Instruments

Since there are probably about three hundred and fifty different Indian tribes, it is difficult to speak of Indian music in general terms. There is no doubt that each tribe has its own musical heritage.

However, most, if not all, Indian tribes have used the drum in signaling, in ceremonies and to accompany dancing and, in some cases, singing. In addition to drums, flutes, whistles, and rattles are common to most Indian music.

Different kinds of drums are hand drums made of skins and bark, tom-toms, immense drums with several men playing, and water drums, kegs partially filled with water. Flutes range from one tone to those with several pitches. Whistles vary with the kind of materials used, tree branches, cane, leaves, etc. Rattles are associated with religious occasions and other ceremonies. These vary from objects filled with small pebbles to sticks with small objects suspended from one end. Indians also use wooden clappers and notched sticks.

The drum, the most basic of instruments, is attractive to all children.

DRUMMING TO INDIAN MUSIC

Grades: 1 – 6

Focus: Exploring drum sounds; Playing a drum accompaniment to "The Navajo Happy Song."

Materials: Any drums available.

Procedure:

- Learn to sing the song.
- Emphasize the accent on count one.
- Gather all available drums.
- Using the fingers and palms of your hands, slap out even rhythms on each drum several times.
- Organize the drums by pitch, from the highest to the lowest.

The Navajo Happy Song

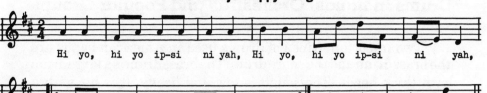

Hi yo, hi yo ip-si ni yah, Hi yo, hi yo ip-si ni yah,

Hi yo, Hi yo, ip-si ni – yah ip – si ni Yah!

Drums in Bands, Orchestras and Popular Groups

Two important kinds of drums used in American bands are the brass drum and the snare drum. The brass drum is a large drum with thick heads. The sound is low and heavy. It is hit with a padded mallet. The snare drum, or side drum, is a smaller drum with the two heads stretched over a cylindrical metal shell. The player strikes the upper head with two hardwood drum sticks. The lower head is thinner and has tight strings something like violin strings stretched across it. When the upper head is struck, the metal strings, called snares, vibrate on the lower head and make a brilliant sound.

Symphony orchestras and concert bands use tympani or kettledrums, shaped like big kettles with heads stretched over the top. These can be tuned to different pitches. A tune can be played with two or more tympani. All the sounds are in a very low register.

Bongo drums are small attached sets of two, sometimes more, drums. The player sometimes holds them between the knees and plays them with the fingers and palms.

Drum sets with more than one drum and cymbals and sometimes other attachments are used in dance groups.

Children may make drums from cardboard cartons, barrels and stretched heads, wooden bowls and other objects with a resonating chamber and some kind of a tight head to strike.

PARADE DRUMS

Grades: K – 3

Focus: Gathering, exploring, and testing and improvising on drums; Preparing for a patriotic parade.

Materials: Any available drums or potential drum material; Recorded march.

Procedure:

- Use as many drums as possible. Let the ensemble play marching music (left-right) on their drums. Direct them to keep together.
- Repeat, all drums being played with hands.
- Repeat, all drums being played with some kind of mallet.

- Give each drummer a turn to demonstrate the drum.
- Divide the drums into two groups—low-loud and high-soft.
- Play the drums; first one group, then the other.
- Listen to a recording of a march. "The Stars and Stripes Forever" is a good one.
- Repeat the record with drum playing. Direct the drum groups according to the soft and loud parts of the record.
- All children march and play drums.

Improvise other drums from cartons and cans (no sharp edges), and mallets from rhythm sticks, pencils, twigs, spoons, etc.

Enrichment:

Use the same recording; direct each drummer across the room and back to his/her seat while another drummer follows. In quick succession all drummers have an opportunity to march and play a solo.

Related Activities:

- Invite a drummer to give a demonstration.
- Listen to the high school band.
- Gather information concerning city, college, or other band performances. Encourage children and parents to attend.

The Appalachian Dulcimer
(Plucked Dulcimer)

The Appalachian or plucked dulcimer is a folk instrument from the Eastern and Southern parts of the United States. A handmade instrument, it probably developed from string instruments brought from Europe by the early Scottish, English, Irish, Dutch, and German settlers. This may account for the lack of standardization in size, playing techniques and notation.

The dulcimer is a good instrument for American children. It lends itself not only to the playing of American folk music, but also to use in performing and recording current music.

The dulcimer has a melody string (sometimes doubled) and two other strings for a drone accompaniment, somewhat like a bagpipe. With practice, chords can also be played on the dulcimer. Most songs associated with the dulcimer are modal. The dulcimer may be tuned to any mode but the Ionian (major), Mixolydian, Aeolian (natural minor), and Dorian are the most used. Although it is a simple instrument to play, the implications and potentials of the instrument have made the dulcimer the subject of several scholarly musicological studies.

The dulcimer is played with a noter, a piece of wooden doweling or cane 4" or 5" long and about ⅜" in diameter. The noter is held in the left hand with the thumb on top and the index finger below to guide the noter. It is placed just to the left of the fret to be sounded on the melody string, the string nearest the player.

Ionian or Major Tuning

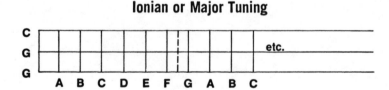

To Tune to the Piano

Hold the dulcimer on your lap, one hand on the peg, the other hand plucking the string as you turn the peg, pressing slightly as you tune. Play C on the piano and sustain the tone

with the right pedal while you listen and tune the bass string.
Repeat this process for the other two strings.

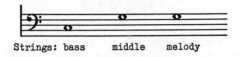

THE DULCIMER

Lesson One

Grades: 2 – 8 (For younger children, the teacher will tune).

Focus: Sitting, holding, strumming, noting.

Materials: One or more dulcimers.

Procedure:

- Sit on a low stool or an armless chair.
- Hold the dulcimer on your lap, tuning pegs on your left, the other end pulled toward your right hip for balance. Some dulcimer players tilt the dulcimer and strum it like a guitar.
- Hold a pick between your right thumb and index finger and strum away from you over the sound-hollow. The most common strum is "Bum, bid-dy bum," adapted to the meter of the piece. Play this.
- Hold the noter just to the left of the third fret. Strum. This is middle C (in the Ionian tuning). (Bum, bid-dy bum)
- Strum without the noter. This is low G.
- Strum with the noter to the left of fret 1. This is A.
- Strum with the noter to the left of fret 2. This is B.
- Once more, note the third fret (C).
- Play G A B D.
- Note fret 4. This is D.
- Note fret 5. This is E.
- Note fret 6. This is F.
- Note fret 7. This is G.
- Explore the pitches by noting different frets.

THE DULCIMER

Lesson Two

Focus: Playing simple melodies.

Procedure:

- Fret the melody string on the following frets, at the same time strumming on each one "Bum, bid-dy bum".

    3 1 3 4 7 4 5 4 3 0 1 3 1 0

- Practice this sequence until you can slide the noter easily from one fret to another. You may hear the slide. This is natural.

- Play "Yonder She Comes"

Yonder She Comes

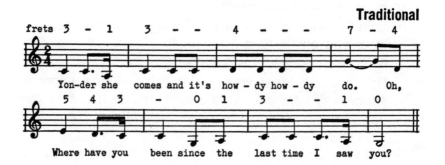

Enrichment:

- Play the dulcimer as an accompaniment for class singing of "Yonder She Comes."

- Make up other question verses for the song.

The Guitar

Guitar-like instruments in various shapes and sizes existed in the Orient around the thirteenth century. In the sixteenth and seventeenth centuries, similar instruments with different names were known in Europe. In the eighteenth century, the English used a kind of guitar. The Portuguese guitar was the ancestor of the ukulele. In Russia they still have the balalaika. In Spain and Mexico guitars have been popular for many years.

In America there are several kinds of guitars in use today—classical, folk, twelve-string, arch-top, electric-acoustic. Each is particularly good for certain kinds of music like concert, informal chording, country, dance band, rock.

The folk guitar is the most widely used guitar. It is also the best kind of instrument for beginners and for informal use. It has six strings tuned E, A, D, G, B, and E. Just strumming the open strings makes a pleasant sound. After learning a few chords you can accompany many simple songs. With a knowledge of more chords, the names of the frets, and fingerings, you can play more difficult music. The folk guitar is associated with cowboy music. It is also used by folk and country singers, professional entertainers, children and other people who just like to make music.

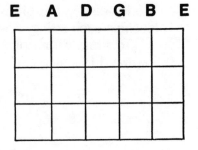

THE GUITAR

Lesson One

Grades: 3 – 8

Focus: Tuning, Holding, Strumming; The D major chord.

Materials: One or more guitars, picks.

Procedure:

Tuning to the Piano
(See the lesson on tuning the ukulele
for more suggestions)

Play the low E on the piano. Match the pitch of the E string (the one on the left) (6th string).

Tune in succession the A, D, G, B, and high E strings.

Holding the Guitar

As you sit, anchor the guitar body on your right knee, hold your right hand over the sound hole ready to strum. Put your left hand around the upper neck, ready to finger the fret board.

Strumming

The thumb brush is easy to strum with for beginners.

Keeping a flexible wrist, quickly bring your thumb downward touching each string. Keep a steady rhythm.

To strum with a pick, hold the pick firmly and guide the point downward touching each string.

THE GUITAR

Lesson Two

Focus: The D major chord, A_7 chord; Accompanying familiar songs.

Procedure:

The index finger is finger 1.

D Major Chord

Put finger 1 before fret 2 on the G string; finger 2 before fret 2 on the E string; finger 3 before fret 3 on the B string.

- Start strumming on the A string. Do not strum the low E string (X).
- Strum with the thumb brush.
- Strum with a pick.
- Hum or sing "Row, Row, Row Your Boat" as you strum the beat.

A7 Chord

- Put finger 1 before fret 2 on the D string; finger 2 before fret 2 on the B string.
- Strum either with thumb brush or pick.
- Practice fingering without strumming—fingers on, off.
- Practice fingering the D chord, the A7 chord, alternating.
- Finger the chords and strum, first one then the other.
- Hum or sing "Row, Row, Row Your Boat." This time play the A7 chord on "Life is but" then play D on the word "dream."

nrichment:

Here are some songs to accompany with the D and A7 chords.

He's Got the Whole Word in His Hands

Rock-a-My Soul

Skip to My Lou

Down in the Valley

On Top of Old Smoky

Get Along Little Dogies

Oh, When the Saints Go Marching In

Michael, Row the Boat Ashore

Bow Belinda

I Had a Cat

Mary Had a Little Lamb

Clementine

Rig-a-jig-jig

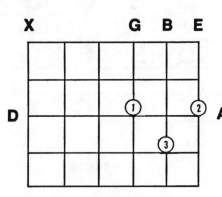
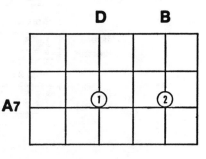

The Harmonica

This little instrument, sometimes called the "pocket piano," is one of the least expensive and most popular recreational instruments in the world. In addition to the thousands of boys and girls who carry a harmonica, at least three United States presidents are known to have played it—Abraham Lincoln, Calvin Coolidge, and Dwight D. Eisenhower. Settlers and cowboys carried it with them across the plains. Soldiers and sailors sometimes take a harmonica along for company. The rhythm and blues groups of the sixties used the harmonica in wild offbeat effects.

The harmonica is probably a descendent of the pentatonic Chinese Sheng invented about 4500 years ago. When it was brought to Europe it went through several developments until, in the mid-nineteenth century, a German clockmaker named Mathias Hohner designed it as we know it today.

Although there are several models with extended ranges, the ten-hole diatonic harmonica is the basic instrument. Using the holes 4, 5, 6, and 7 on a harmonica tuned in C, you can play the complete C major scale and many familiar melodies. Each hole produces two tones. Blow for one; draw for the other.

TEN (SINGLE) HOLE HARMONICA

Tablature

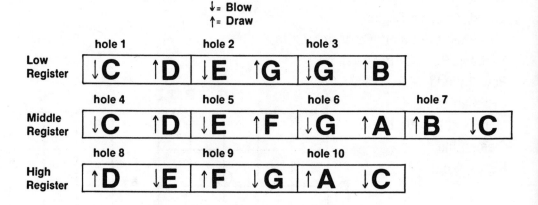

Notation

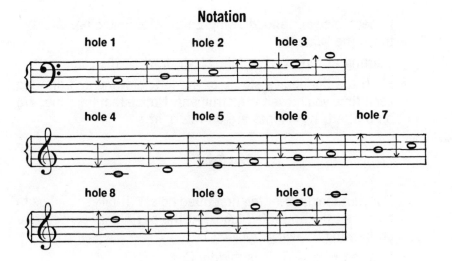

THE HARMONICA

(This lesson may be divided into two parts, depending on how fast the students progress)

Grades: 3 – 8

Focus: Learning the tablature; Blowing and drawing; Playing in the middle register.

Materials: Each student must have his/her own harmonica (ten hole).

Procedure:

Part One

Directions to give . . . (Check each position and step of the lesson.)

- Hold the harmonica in the left hand, thumb on the bottom, first two fingers flat on the top.
- Put it to your mouth and blow gently.
- Draw gently.

- Repeat blowing and drawing.Emphasize listening. Are the tones the same?
- Starting at the extreme left, blow; draw on the same hole.
- Move the harmonica slowly to the left, blowing and drawing each time you move the instrument. Notice that low tones are on the left, high tones are on the right.

Part Two

- Put your tongue over the first three holes. (It takes practice to block out the unwanted tones. At the beginning, concentrate on blowing, drawing, moving.)
- Blow on hole 4. This is middle C.
- Play this several times.
- Draw on the same hole. This is D.
- Move the harmonica slightly to the left and blow on hole 5. This is E.
- Draw on the same hole. This is F.
- Move the harmonica again and blow hole 6. This is G.
- Draw on the same hole. This is A.
- The next hole, 7, is different.
- *Draw* on hole 7 for the next tone, B.
- *Blow* on hole 7 for the high C.

Enrichment:

Encourage home and playground practice. Concentrate on the moving to the right for higher tones.

Related Activities:

- Invite a harmonica player to demonstrate.
- Find recordings that include the harmonica.

Keyboards

Keyboards likely to be available to today's students include the traditional piano, electric piano, and several kinds of organs. The easy American folk tunes used here may be played and harmonized on any keyboard. After completing these keyboard lessons, students will have a basic knowledge of keyboard topography and should be encouraged to expand their knowledge of notation and chords.

The center of the keyboard is the singing range of most people. Chords are generally played one octave lower. When fingering the keyboard, the thumb is always finger one, the index finger, 2, etc. Keep your hand in one convenient fingering position throughout the phrase whenever possible.

THE KEYBOARD

Lesson One
(May be presented in two or three sections)

Grades: 3 – 8

Focus: Black and White Keys; "Merrily We Roll Along."

Materials: One or more keyboard.

When only one keyboard is used, students take turns playing. Each student can make his/her own paper keyboard for practice. A keyboard chart is useful for demonstration.

Procedure:

"Merrily We Roll Along" (four tone melody)

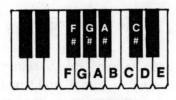

On Four Black Keys

A#G# F# G#A# - - G# - - A#C#
Mer-ri-ly we roll a-long, roll a-long, roll a-long

A#G# F# G#A# - - G# - A#G#F#
Mer-ri-ly we roll a-long, on the bright blue sea.

- Find a set of three and two black keys in the middle of the keyboard.
- Arrange the right hand—fingers 1 (F#), 2, 3, and 5—on the keys needed for the song.
- Play each black key as it appears in the song. Speak the key name.
- Repeat. Play the keys, thinking, humming, or singing the melody.
- Students take turn playing while the others sing.

On Four White Keys
(Key of F)

- Move fingers down to the *left* to play the adjacent white keys.
- Play the melody again on the white keys. It will sound lower.
- Repeat, singing the key names (F G A C).
- Play again, thinking, humming or singing the melody.

On Four White Keys
(Key of G)

- Play the melody on the black keys.
- Move fingers up to the *right* to the adjacent white keys (G A B D). (The distance from one key to an adjacent key is called a half step.)

- Play the melody starting on B.
- Students take turn playing while others sing.

Enrichment:

Transpose lower to the key of C (C D E G); to the key of D (D E F♯ A). Play starting on each of the twelve keys.

Related Activities:

Combine the keyboard with the playing of other melody instruments such as the recorder.

THE KEYBOARD

Lesson Two
(May be presented in three or four sections)

Focus: Learning two chords for the left hand (F and C₇) (G and C₇); Playing the chords with "Merrily We Roll Along" in the key of F; G.

Procedure:

In the Key of F

F Chord	finger	C₇ Chord	finger
C	1	C	1
A	3	B♭	2
F	5	E	5

```
    F  /   /   /   C₇  /    F  /
Merrily we roll along, roll along, roll along,
    F  /   /   /   C₇   /      F  /
Merrily we roll along, on the dark blue sea.
```

- With the left hand, finger the F chord.
- Play this as you sing the first phrase of "Merrily We Roll Along."
- Finger the C₇ chord.
- Bounce your fingers on the C₇ chord until you feel it in your finger tips.

- Play the F chord. Change to C₇. Change back to F. Repeat slowly.
- Play the chords again as you sing the song, changing the chords as indicated over the words.
- Students take turns playing chords as others sing.
- With the right hand, play the melody in the key of F (starts on A).
- Play the F and C₇ chords with the left hand.
- Play the melody and chords together.
- Students take turns playing for singing.

In the Key of G

G Chord	finger	D7 Chord	finger
D	1	D	1
B	3	C	2
G	5	F#	5

- With the left hand, finger the G chord.
- Play this as you sing the first phrase of the song.
- Finger the D₇ chord.
- Bounce your fingers on the D₇ chord.
- Play the G chord. Move to the D₇ chord, then back to G. Repeat this several times.
- As you think, hum or sing the song, keep time, changing the chords as indicated.
- Students take turns playing chords as others sing.
- With the right hand, play the melody in the key of G (starts on B).
- With the left hand, play the chords, G and D₇.
- Play the melody and chords together.
- Play for singing.

THE KEYBOARD
Lesson Three
(May be presented in two or three sections)

Focus: Learning the keyboard; Playing "Old Brass Wagon" (5 tone melody) on the black keys. Transposing "Old Brass Wagon" to the key of F (white keys).

Procedure:

F♯   /   /   D♯ C♯
Cir-cle to the right, the old brass wag-on,

G♯   /   C♯   D♯ F♯
Cir-cle to the right, the old brass wag-on,

A♯   /   G♯ F♯   D♯ F♯
Cir-cle to the right, the old brass wag-on,

G♯   A♯ C♯   D♯ F♯
You-re the one my dar-ling.

- Find a set of two and three black keys in the middle of the keyboard.
- Put your right fingers over the five black keys.
- Play the keys in succession as they occur in the melody. Repeat several times.
- Play the keys again, thinking, humming, or singing the words of the song.
- Students take turns playing for singing.

In the Key of F

- Play "Old Brass Wagon" on the black keys.
- Move all fingers down to the left to adjacent white keys.
- Play the melody again on the white keys. (F, not F♯), (G not G♯), etc.

In the Key of G

- Play "Old Brass Wagon" in the key of F.
- Move all fingers up to the right to the white keys.
- Play the melody again. Start on G.
- Play for singing.

Enrichment:

- Play the melody with the left hand, on the black keys.
- Finger keys with left fingers.
- Play in the key of F; in G.

THE KEYBOARD

Lesson Four
(May be presented in three or four sections)

Focus: Learning a third chord; (B♭ (IV) for key of F and C (IV) for the key of G); Using three chords with "Old Brass Wagon."

Procedure:

In the Key of F

F chord	B♭ chord	finger	C7 chord
C	D	1	C
A	B♭	2	B♭
F	F	5	E

- Play the F chord.
- Move to B♭ chord. (Notice that F is in both chords.)
- Practice moving slowly from F to B♭ to C7 to F chords.

F   / / /
Circle to the right, the old brass wagon.

C7   / F /
Circle to the right, the old brass wagon,

F   / F /
Circle to the right, the old brass wagon,

C7   / F /
You're the one my darling.

- As you think, hum, or sing the song, keep time with chords, change as indicated over the words.
- Students take turns playing for singing.
- Play the melody in the key of F with the right hand.
- Play the new chord sequence with the left hand.

- Play the melody and chords together.
- Students take turns playing for singing.

In the Key of G

G chord	C chord	finger	D$_7$ chord
D	E	1	D
B	C	2	C
G	G	5	F$\sharp$

- Play the G chord.
- Move to the C chord. (Note that G is in both chords.)
- Practice moving slowly from G to C to D$_7$ to G.
- Bounce each chord several times before moving.
- As you think, hum, or sing the song, keep time with the chords, changing as indicated over the words.
- Students take turns playing for singing.
- With your right hand, play the melody in the key of G. (Start on G.)
- With the left hand play the chords as they occur in the song.
- Play the melody and chords together.
- Students take turns playing for singing.

The Recorder

Whistles and simple wind instruments are common to all times and cultures. Whistle (fipple) flutes, or recorders as we know them, were an important part of late Renaissance music in Europe. They were brought to America by early settlers. In some isolated settlements, especially in the Appalachian mountains, recorders were handmade.

There are four sizes of recorders, paralleling the vocal quartet, soprano, alto, tenor, and bass. The soprano, sounding one octave higher than the notation, is the most common. It is especially popular with young people because it can be played by small hands.

Listening Materials

1. English Renaissance Music
   Recorder Consorts
   Madrigals by William Byrd (1543 – 1623)
   Some of the five or six voice parts were often played on recorders as well as lutes or guitars.

2. Anglo-American Ballads (2037 – Folkways)
   The melodies of these songs were probably played on recorders by Americans from England.

3. Contemporary recorder music such as *Gesti* (1966) for alto recorder solo by Luciano Berio

THE RECORDER
(Soprano)
Lesson One

Grades: 3 (or when second teeth are in) – 8

Focus: Beginning techniques for playing; Fingering the recorder.

Materials: Each student should have his/her hardwood or plastic instrument. If these beginning lessons are used as demonstrations, each student may use a long wooden pencil or rhythm stick to learn fingering until instruments are available.

Procedure:

Thumb hole	Fingers	
O	O 1	
	O 2	**Left hand**
	O 3	

	Fingers	
	O 1	
	O 2	**Right hand**
O O	3	
O O	4	

The recorder is made of two parts, a head with the mouthpiece and window and a body with the thumb and finger holes. (The head alone is an ordinary whistle.) The two parts fit snugly together. (If the recorder tunes sharp, loosen it slightly.)

To hold the recorder, sit up straight, elbows held loosely from the shoulders. Hold the recorder in the left hand, thumb over the thumb hole on the back. Cover hole 1 (top) with finger 1 (index finger), hole 2 with finger 2, and hole 3 with finger 3.

Put the right hand fingers over the succeeding holes 4, 5, 6, 7, (holes 6 and 7 are often double holes) with fingers 1 (index), 2, 3, 4. Use the cushions of the fingers to fully cover the holes and to prevent leaks.

To Begin Playing

- Open your mouth slightly and put the mouthpiece of the re-corder on your lower lip in front of your teeth. Then close your mouth so that no air excapes. Relax your mouth.

- With your tongue in back of your upper teeth, form a silent "too."

- Blow gently into the recorder. (Blowing too hard will change the pitch.)

- Without blowing, think through each finger, feeling the cushion on each hole.

- Take right hand finger 4 off hole. Blow gently.
- Take right hand finger 3 off hole. Blow gently.
- Take right hand finger 2 off hole. Blow gently.
- Take right hand finger 1 off hole. Continue to support the recorder with your right hand. Blow gently. This is G, the tone we start with in the next lesson.

THE RECORDER

Lesson Two

Focus: Review of holding, fingering, blowing techniques; Playing G, A, B and three-tone melodies.

Procedure:

- Hold the recorder in the left hand, holes covered. Support it with your right hand.
- Put the recorder in your mouth ready to blow.
- Check that the holes are covered by thinking through the cushions of your fingers. Finger G (Holes covered—1, 2, 3, and thumb hole).
- Blow gently. Sustain the tone. Listen.
- Tongue behind teeth, blow "too." End the tone by pressing the tongue against the teeth "t."
- Finger A.
- Play "too . . . t."
- Finger B
- Play "too . . . t."
- Play G A B A G with long sustained tones.
- Play the melodies below. The second one is familiar. Finish it by ear.

Enrichment:

- Play these progressions
  A B A B A B G . . . B A B A B A G
- Play your own tunes.

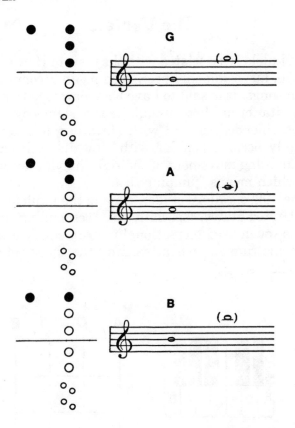

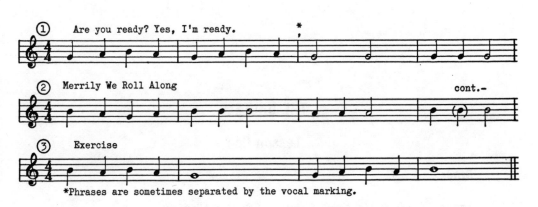

*Phrases are sometimes separated by the vocal marking.

The Ukulele

The ukulele is associated with the state of Hawaii and, since about 1880, has commonly been used as an accompaniment for Hawaiian songs. It is said to have been developed from the Portuguese guitar or machete brought to the islands by sailors. This instrument blended so well with Hawaiian folk songs that it immediately became popular with Hawaiians. Because of the jerky strumming movement of the right hand, they called it the ukulele which means "jumping flea."

In the 1920s, college students made the ukulele popular all over the United States, especially as a "serenading" instrument. It is still a much used recreational instrument. It is also a good "teaching instrument" when learning the theory of scales and common chords.

 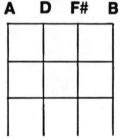

THE UKULELE

Lesson One

Grades: 4 – 8

Focus: Tuning; Holding; Plucking; Strumming.

Materials: One or more ukuleles; Chart with names of strings (or draw on the chalk board); Keyboard or other chromatic instrument for tuning.

Procedure:

Tuning with the Piano

- Hold the ukulele in your lap with the tuning pegs up.
- Play middle A (above middle C) on the piano. Immediately press down the right (sostenuto) pedal to sustain the A sound.
- Pluck the A string (left on the fret board).
- Tighten the A string for higher pitch and loosen it for lower pitch to match the A on the piano. Repeat the tuning routine if needed.
- Play middle D (Next to middle C) on the piano. Sustain it with the pedal. Pluck the D string (next to A) and match the tone.
- Play middle F♯ on the piano. Tune the ukulele as before.
- Repeat the tuning routine for B string.

Tuning by Ear

After you have memorized the sounds of the open strings, you will be able to tune your ukulele by ear. This is called approximate tuning because it may not be exactly on pitch. Tuning by ear is important when a keyboard is not available.

- Sing or think A as you remember it and tighten or loosen the A string to match. (Hints—If it is too loose it will sound dull. If it is too tight it will sound brittle with no "ring." Also, it might break.)
- Some people sing this ditty to help them tune by ear. "My (A) dog (D) has (F♯) fleas (B)."
- If you have a low voice and intend to sing with your own accompaniment, tune the A a little lower.

Tuning with the Guitar
(E̲ A D G B E̅)

- Tune the ukulele A string an octave higher than the guitar A string.

- Match the two D strings.
- Tune the F♯ by ear or have the guitarist play F♯ .
- Match the B strings. This tuning is essential when the two instruments are being played together and a piano is not available.

Holding the Ukulele

Hold the neck of the ukulele with the left hand, thumb underneath, palm of hand away from neck and fingers above (ready to finger the frets).

Plucking the Strings

Use your right thumb to pluck the strings in a downward motion or pluck the A string with the thumb, the D string with finger 1 (index finger), F♯ with finger 2, and B with finger 3.

- Pluck this ditty.

```
A    A    A    A    D    D    D    D   F♯  F♯  F♯  F♯
My, my, my, my; dog, dog, dog, dog; has, has, has, has;
 B    B    B    B
fleas, fleas, fleas, fleas.
```

- Repeat it with your own rhythmic variations.

Strumming

- Hold your right hand down limp.
- Let the tip of finger 1 touch the strings.
- Swing from the wrist and strum the strings over the sound hole.
- Strum DOWN up, DOWN up. DOWN up, DOWN up.
- Strum your version of the ditty above.

Enrichment:

Other ditties for tuning and improvising, or to use as a song:

"Fleas make dogs wheeze,"
"Fleas like to tease;"
"Fleas don't bite bees,"
"Bees! Fleas flee bees."

POOR DOG!

Related Activities:

Learn the name of the chord you strum with open strings, a D_6 chord. (D F# A B).

THE UKULELE

Lesson Two

Focus: Fingering the frets; playing D_7 and G chords.

Procedure:

- Press finger 1 (index finger) before fret one on B string.
- Strum. This is the D_7 chord.
- Strum open strings (D_6); strum D_7. Practice strumming and moving from one chord to the other.
- To finger the G chord, put finger 1 before fret one on F# string, finger 2 before fret two on the A string. Strum.
- Practice moving from G to D_7 chord.
- Play and sing "Ain't Gonna Rain."

Enrichment:

- Learn the C chord. Practice G, D_7 and C chords.
- Accompany "Aloha Oe."

G	D₇	C

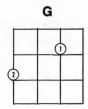 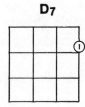 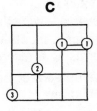

Whistling, Whistles, and the Fife

Whistling is accomplished by forcing your breath through a small opening in your mouth. Purse your lips and blow through your teeth. Help the whistle by putting your tongue behind your teeth or against your lower lip.

A whistling sound may be made by blowing through or over the end of a tube or pipe. This is a *Whistle*. Some people make whistles from twigs and branches and sometimes from folded leaves.

A *Fife* is a kind of whistle with six to eight finger holes to shorten or lengthen the tube and produce different pitches. (The recorder is also a kind of whistle.) The fife sounds like a high pitched flute. It was used extensively in early American Fife and Drum Corps for marching. The fife played the melody while the drum kept the beat. In more recent times the piccolo has become more generally used with the drum.

WHISTLING

Grades: 1 – 3

Focus: Whistling "Yankee Doodle."

Materials: (Optional) Recording of Yankee Doodle.

Procedure:

- Sing "Yankee Doodle" (or listen to recording). (If children know the melody of "Yankee Doodle" skip this step.)
- Sing or whistle the first part of "Yankee Doodle" to establish the key.
- Everyone whistle "Yankee Doodle." Direct the ensemble by singing, mouthing the words, using hand motions, whistling, or using a recording.
- Volunteers or best whistlers may demonstrate for the other children.
- Whistle "This Old Man" and other familiar songs.

Enrichment:

- Make a continuing list of songs to whistle. This may also serve the purpose of recording the class repertoire.

- Combine the whistling of "Yankee Doodle" with chording played on the autoharp, keyboard, guitar, or ukulele. (Chords are indicated above the melody.)

Yankee Doodle

Eighteenth Century

O fath'r and I went down to camp, along with Captain Good'in,
And there we saw the men and boys as thick as hasty puddin'.

Yankee Doodle keep it up, Yankee Doodle Dandy,
Mind the music and the step, And with the girls be handy.

Informal Instruments

BONES

The history of the percussion instrument, bones, is a long one. They have been found in excavations in Mesopotamia; pictures of them appear on Egyptian vases from 3000 B.C.; and the ancient Greeks used them in certain religious ceremonies. In the middle ages, wandering minstrels used them to accompany their dancing and singing. There are also records of their early use in Northern Europe. In Latin America, the claves, used in dance bands, are similar.

In nineteenth century America, bones were associated with street bands and minstrel shows. In contemporary America they are used by Blue Grass and Country Music groups, as well as by informal gatherings of friends making music.

Real bones are slightly curved, bleached and polished rib bones of sheep or cattle. Wooden bones may be purchased or made. Hardwood bones have a brittle tone, softwood, a more mellow sound. Bones are generally about 7 or 7½ inches long and less than an inch wide. Any size that fits well in your hands may be used.

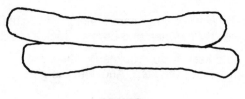

BONES

Lesson One

Grades: 4 – 8

Focus: Gathering materials; Making bones.

Materials: Strips of hardwood or softwood 7″ to 7½″ long, ¾″ to 1″ wide, and ½″ to ¾″ thick, or beef rib bones of the same length. Substitutes may be 6″ rulers or tongue depressors.

Procedure:

Each student needs one pair. Some bone players use a pair in each hand.

Wooden Bones

- After the strips are cut to 7½" for large hands, 7" for average hands, or 6½" for children, the ends should be rounded. This may be done with coarse sandpaper or by whittling. (Whittling should be done only at the discretion of the teacher.)
- To make the bones convex, sand or whittle the center to about ⅜" thickness.

Animal Bones

- Have beef rib bones cut to the proper lengths.
- Scrape and clean the bones.
- Bleach them in the sun or by other means.
- Dry them well.
- Sand and polish them with sandpaper or emery cloth.

BONES

Lesson Two

Focus: Holding; Playing.

Procedure:

Holding

The bones are held in one hand, convex sides facing each other. Hold the *moving* bone over your palm between the third and fourth fingers. One end extends slightly above the knuckles. The fourth finger presses firmly on the bone and the fifth finger stabilizes the other two fingers.

Hold the *stationary* bone between the second and third fingers. This bone extends a little higher above the knuckles than the other bone. The long end rests on the palm, with the thumb held against the first finger.

Playing

- Extend your arm(s), elbow(s) bent, thumb(s) down.
- With a quick motion, turn your wrist(s) so that your thumb(s) is (are) out. The sound will be a tap.
- Play these rhythms to establish your playing techniques. When you can play these basic exercises, you are ready to create your own rhythms.

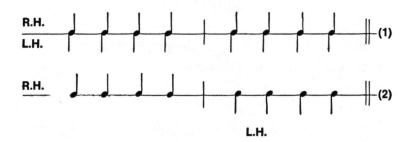

BEGINNING LESSON ON THE JAW HARP

Grades: 3 – 8 (After second front teeth are in)

Focus: Holding; Producing a Sound.

Materials: One jaw harp for each student.

Procedure:

How to Play

Hold the jaw harp lightly in your left hand with the index finger around the top curve of the frame and the thumb around the bottom. (Fingers must not touch the vibrator.) The trigger points away from you.

With your mouth slightly open, gently press your upper teeth on the slanting bevel of the upper frame and your lower teeth on the lower bevel.

With your right index finger, stroke the trigger away from you horizontally. (Stroke it back and forth for rhythmic variations.) Breathe in and out in rhythm "Ah, ha, ah, ha." Keep your tongue away from the vibrator.

Your mouth is the resonating chamber with your tongue controlling the size. (Moving the tongue up makes the cavity smaller and the pitch higher.)

Notation for Strokes

$$x = \quad \oslash = \quad \oslash. = \quad \infty = \circ$$

- Check holding positions after each step.
- Hold the jaw harp in your left hand.
- Set it in your mouth.
- Practice stroking the trigger.
- Breathe in and out as you stroke the trigger.
- Think the melody of "This Old Man" or another familiar song and stroke the rhythm of the song.

This Old Man

Traditional

Enrichment:

Most children will need further individual practice. Encourage playground and home playing and experimenting.

Other songs to accompany:

Goodbye Old Paint

Bought Me a Cat

Ain't Gonna' Rain

Home on the Range

Red River Valley

O Susanna

Related Activities:

- Listen to recordings of a Blue Grass group using the jaws' harp.
- Invite a jaws' harp player to demonstrate.

THE JUG

Jug bands were very popular during the '20s and consisted of almost anything that sounded—washboards, saws, kazoos, spoons and bones. Fiddles, mandolins, banjos and guitars might also be part of these bands.

There were country jug bands playing for dances and playing blues. City bands played Dixieland jazz or whatever kind of jazz was popular at the time.

In the great folk revival of the '60s, jug band music again became popular, mostly for recreation.

THE JUG — LESSON

Grades: 4 – 8

Focus: Finding a jug; Playing your jug.

Materials: a jug of glass, stoneware, plastic, ceramic or a bottle with a narrow mouth. (Different sizes of jugs and bottles make different sounds and pitches.)

Procedure:

- To hold your jug, put a finger through the loop handle on the neck and hold it below your mouth.
- Rest it under your lower lip (like a flute).
- Pucker your lips and blow across and into the jug. The sound will be low like a fog horn.

- Vary the sound by blowing with short puffs or moving your tongue as you blow.
- Practice with your jug or bottle until you can make the jug sound and produce at least one variation.
- Play an accompaniment to a familiar song, preferably with the help of an autoharp, guitar or other instrument.

Enrichment:

- Play your jug with a Dixieland Jazz record.
- Listen to *Jim Kweskin and the Jug Band,* Vanguard VRS 9139 and VSD 2158.

THE KAZOO

The kazoo is a metal tube about 5" long, tapering from the ¾" mouth end to less than ½" at the other end. On the top side is a hole covered with a thin, stretched skin for a vibrator. This amplifies your voice as you hum into it.

It is probably the one instrument everyone can play. It is also a very inexpensive instrument.

KAZOO — LESSON

Grades: 1 – 8

Focus: Playing the kazoo; Playing "Oh! Susanna."

Materials: Each student should have his/her own kazoo.

Procedure:

To Play

1. Sing "who" with full breath into the larger or mouth end of the kazoo (head singing).
2. Sing "too" into the mouth end (tongue singing).

Playing "Oh! Susanna"

1. Sing with "who."
2. Repeat with "too."

Enrichment:

Children take turns choosing familiar melodies to play.

Related Activities:

Fold a piece of tissue paper over a comb and sing over it. The resulting sound will be similar to the "zoo" sound.

THE WASHTUB BASS
(Gut Bucket or Thumper)

Lesson One

This should be a demonstration lesson or should be done by students under authorized supervision.

Grades: 6 – 8

Focus: Making a washtub bass.

Materials: Galvanized steel washtub, bass catgut G string or 4 to 6 ft. of nylon-wrapped cord, one eye bolt, 2 nuts, 2–4 washers, 4 ft. broom handle or similar pole. (Tools: hammer, screwdriver, drill.)

Procedure:

- Remove handles. Pound holes smooth.
- Drill a hole or drive a large nail through the center of the tub.
- Put one or two washers, one nut, and the end of an eye bolt through the hole.
- Drill a small hole near one end of the pole.
- On the other end of the pole cut a notch to fit over the lip of the tub. This stabilizes the pole during playing.
- Tie one end of the string securely in the eye bolt.
- Set the pole upright in playing position to measure the string length.
- Tie the other end of the string in the hole in the pole. Make it taut.

Enrichment:

Listen to *Jug Band Music,* Vanguard VRS 3159

WASHTUB BASS

Lesson Two

Grades: 4 – 8

Focus: Playing

Materials: One or more washtub basses.

Procedure:

- Stand in back of the pole.
- Hold the pole upright with the notch on the lip of the tub.
- Pull the string back toward the pole with the left hand. This is fretting.
- Pluck the string with the right hand.
- Fret the string and pull the pole back at the same time.
- Slap the string. (These techniques are the most common ways of varying the pitch. Slapping and plucking bring out the sound, the characteristic "boing.")
- Explore these techniques.
- Play an accompaniment to a familiar song.

Enrichment:

- Listen to *The Jug Bands,* Folkways FR Records
- Play an accompaniment to the recording.

PART THREE

Listening to American Music

FAMOUS COMPOSERS AND ENTERTAINERS

"Maple Leaf Rag" — Joplin

"St. Louis Blues" — Handy

"Sophisticated Lady" — Duke Ellington

Benny Goodman and the Swing Era

"Blue Rondo a la Turk" — Brubeck

THE BAND

"Semper Fideles"

Children's March

Bugles and Drums

PIANO

"La Bamboula"

"To a Water Lily"

"Juba Dance"

"Banshee"

Prelude II

Largo from Evocations

MUSICAL THEATER

Show Boat; "Ol' Man River"

Oklahoma

Bye Bye Birdie; "Put on a Happy Face"

Amahl and the Night Visitors; "March of the Three Kings"

THE SYMPHONY ORCHESTRA

The Children's Symphony

Merry Mount Suite

"Humor"

PROGRAM MUSIC

"Chester" from New England Triptych

"Father of Waters" from The Mississippi Suite

117

VARIATIONS

Variations on America
American Salute

MUSIC FOR FILM

"Dream March and Circus
Music"
"Acadian Songs and Dances;
"Walking Song" and "The
Squeeze Box"

CHAMBER MUSIC

Allegro from Trio in A Minor
Suite for Wind Quintet

ELECTRONIC MUSIC

A Piece for Tape Recorder
Composition for Synthesizer
Aria with Fontana Mix

Famous Composers and Entertainers

MAPLE LEAF RAG
by
Scott Joplin

Grades: 4 – 8

Focus: Ragtime and Scott Joplin

Materials: *Piano Rags by Scott Joplin* (Joshua Rifkin, piano, Nonesuch H – 71248) (Folkways FG 3563)

Procedure:

Ragtime was very popular in the United States from 1890 to 1910. Traveling pianists played it in cafés, and, eventually, everybody was playing, dancing, or humming it.

Ragtime moved along at a moderate tempo. The syncopated treble was called "ragged time." The bass line had a steady beat.

Scott Joplin was called the "King of Ragtime." He wrote and played many ragtime pieces. As a young boy in Texarkana, Texas, he taught himself to play the piano. As a teenager he played ragtime in St. Louis and Chicago. He also played cornet in a band and traveled with a singing group.

The "Maple Leaf Rag" is named after a club in Sedalia, Missouri where he lived for some time.

- During the first listening, encourage soft foot-tapping on the steady underbeat.
- Play the recording several times. When the students feel the ragged time, they tap it out with fingers or say "ta, ta, ta" to the melody.
- Encourage recognition of the familiar part A. (How many times do you hear part A?)
- On a third listening, students may outline the form of the piece. (How many parts do you hear in the whole piece?) (A A B B A C C D D) (D has elements of A, B, and C.)

Enrichment:

Ragtime is music of movement. A slow shuffling step coupled with shifting arm and body movements makes a simulated ragtime dance.

Related Activities:

Listen to other Joplin rags. "The Entertainer," which was used in the film *The Sting* is a good one. "The Gladiola Rag" is another famous one.

ST. LOUIS BLUES (1914)
(A Composed Blues)
by
William C. Handy

Grades: 4 – 8

Focus: Blues rhythm; The blues formula.

Materials: Recording (*W. C. Handy Blues,* Folkways 3540).

Procedure:

As a child, W. C. Handy and his friends made music any way they could, singing through fine-toothed combs, using the mouth, hand and foot sounds, sticks or drumming on pans. No doubt, he experienced folk blues in its truest form.

He is sometimes called "The Father of the Blues" because of his popular "St. Louis Blues," "Memphis Blues," and others.

He composed piano blues that became popular as ragtime declined around the beginning of World War I. Like other popular music of the day, his blues used simple harmonies – tonic (I), and dominant (IV and V), especially with the seventh and sometimes the ninth added. Often, the third and seventh of the scale were flatted and sometimes played as block chords.

The duple rhythm was slow and syncopated (accents on the weak beats). The organization of "The St. Louis Blues" consists of a three-line verse in the first section and a four-line unit of sixteen bars in the second section.

- While listening the first time, suggest feeling the basic beat through the toes.
- With the second listening, suggest feeling the weak beats with the fingers. After the rhythm is established, double the speed.
- On another listening, sing the melody with "ta, ta, ta."

Enrichment:

Compare the "St. Louis Blues" with Scott Joplin's "Maple Leaf Rag."

Related Activities:

Listen to other blues by Handy ("Memphis Blues," "Joe Turner").

SOPHISTICATED LADY
Duke Ellington

Grades: 4 – 8

Focus: Duke Ellington, his life and music.

Materials: Recording "Sophisticated Lady" (1933) in *Music of Duke Ellington*, Columbia CCL-558 or "Mood Indigo" (1931) in *Masterpieces by Ellington*, Columbia ML 4418.

Procedure:

Edward "Duke" Ellington studied piano as a child and, in his late teens, had his own dance band. He became famous as a leader of bands that played in night clubs. The best known club was the Cotton Club in New York where he played in the twenties. His music was identified by the "Ellington sound" provided by the talented soloists and the "color" combinations he put together.

He is also distinguished by his larger compositions, a suite called *Black, Brown, and Beige,* and the *Golden Broom and Green Apple* which was premiered by the New York Philharmonic Orchestra in 1965 and which he conducted. The acceptance of his jazz compositions by the world of serious music was a milestone in jazz history.

• Listen to "Sophisticated Lady."

- Discuss the melody and the instrumentation and the special "wa wa" sounds of the clarinets, saxophones, trumpets.
- Compare the sounds of this piece with a recording of a current instrumental group. (A third listening will be necessary for comparison.)

Enrichment:

- Listen to one of the suites mentioned above and compare the concert style of the larger composition with the smaller dance style presented in this lesson.
- Listen to *Black, Brown and Beige* from *Duke Ellington at His Very Best,* RCA LPM 1715; *Black and Tan Fantasy* from *The Best of Duke Ellington and His Famous Orchestra,* Capitol SM 1602

BENNY GOODMAN AND THE SWING ERA

Grades: 4 – 8

Focus: Swing music; Special sounds of the swing orchestra.

Materials: Recording (*Benny Goodman's All-Time Greatest Hits,* Columbia KG 31547).

Procedure:

Duke Ellington's 1931 song, It Don't Mean a Thing If It Ain't Got That Swing," anticipated the swing era. But it was Benny Goodman, with his extensive swing recordings and his nationwide tours, who was the "King of Swing." The unique sounds of his clarinet and his big bands and small combos were sensations in the thirties and forties.

Swing, danceable and singable music, has been called singing jazz, sweet jazz (as opposed to hot jazz), pseudo jazz, white jazz, even anti-jazz. Whatever it was, it had a romantic appeal that lasted until about 1950. Other band leaders of the times brought their own versions of swing. Tommy Dorsey featured large string sections. Harry James had his trumpet; Glenn Miller, his arrangements and an emphasis on saxophones, plus his popular theme song "Moonlight Serenade." Woody Herman's group was voted the best swing band of 1945 by *Down Beat Magazine.*

The Benny Goodman swing band sound was characterized by the solid beat of the rhythm instruments – piano, drum, bass; the melody carried by the brasses and reeds (always a little ahead of the beat); and the famous Goodman clarinet improvisations. "Stompin' at the Savoy" was one of the swing style pieces.

- Discuss the era of swing.
- Listen to the music.
- Discuss the rhythm as related to ballroom dancing and why it might have been called "swing."
- Listen again and keep time with feet, hands, or by swaying.
- Discuss melodies and variations.
- After the third listening, describe this kind of music, or encourage students to give their impressions. Compare swing with the present kind of dance music.

Enrichment:

Compare swing to progressive jazz; to rock.

Related Activities:

- Listen to the Benny Goodman Trio, (RCA Victor 1 pt 17).
- Compare a Benny Goodman swing recording to his playing of the Concerto for Clarinet written by Aaron Copland with Benny Goodman in mind.

BLUE RONDO A LA TURK
by
Dave Brubeck

Grades: 6 – 8

Focus: Progressive jazz as a musical style

Materials: Recording; *Time Out: The Dave Brubeck Quartet,* Columbia CS 8192

Procedure:

Even as a child, pianist-composer Dave Brubeck was interested in improvising. As a young man, he formed his own group and experimented with new sounds and rhythms. He studied with composers Darius Milhaud and Arnold Schoenberg who were using new devices in their music. Milhaud used more than one key at a time and experimented with simultaneous rhythms. Schoenberg wrote music based on tonal rows – a set of twelve tones arranged in a certain way – and developed these into musical compositions.

Dave Brubeck used some of his teachers' devices in his own compositions and performance styles. The result was a kind of progressive jazz with new mixtures of sounds that moved in chord blocks with a counterpoint of melodies and unusual rhythms, often alternating triple and duple.

In 1951, the Dave Brubeck Quartet played at the Black Hawk, a San Francisco club. People came to listen, not to dance. This was a new development in jazz. High school students were so enthusiastic that the club set up a special seating section for them.

Blue Rondo begins with the piano playing the A or returning part of the rondo (A B A C A). A saxophone solo, in a kind of improvisation, is the center of the piece. Then, the music picks up again as the piano enters and the piece grows until the final A part.

- Outline the instrumentation. Discuss music for listening versus music for dancing.
- Listen to the recording.
- Discuss rondo form and the A part.
- On second listening, emphasize the saxophone solo as the heart of the piece.
- Before the third listening, review instrumentation, rondo form, recognition of the A part, listening for different instruments.
- Third listening.

Enrichment:

- Change the rhythmic groupings and accents of "Red River Valley" and "Camptown Races." Clap, sing, step.
- Listen to other pieces on the same recording.
- Listen to recordings of Gerry Mulligan and Miles Davis, outstanding exponents of progressive jazz.

The Band

A band is a large instrumental group made up principally of wind instruments.

The American military band is chiefly brass. It generally consists of twenty-eight musicians: 2 sousaphones, 3 trombones, 3 horns, 1 baritone (euphonium), 5 cornets, 1 trumpet, 5 B♭ clarinets, 1 E♭ clarinet, 1 piccolo, 3 saxophones, 1 snare drum, 1 bass drum, 1 cymbal.

A symphonic or concert band is predominantly woodwinds, sometimes with double basses added.

SEMPER FIDELES
(Always Faithful)
by
John Philip Sousa

Grades: 1 – 8

Focus: What is a band? Analyzing a musical composition.

Materials: Recordings: *Sousa Marches,* Mercury MG-40007; *Famous Marches of Sousa,* London LL 1229, Meet the Instruments Posters, Bowmar no. 123.

Procedure:

John Philip Sousa learned to play piano and violin and experimented with all the band instruments. In his early teens he became an apprentice in the Marine Corps band and also formed his own dance band.

He composed over one hundred marches and is sometimes called "The March King." While he was director of the United States Marine Band, he composed this march and named it for the Marine Corps motto. It became the official march for the Marines and is used for parades and public functions.

The sousaphone, a very large brass horn that plays very low tones, was named after Sousa. The sousaphone plays a counter melody under theme two.

The form (organization) of this piece is: introduction, theme 1 (repeated), theme 2 (repeated), interlude (snare drum), theme 3 (3 times), theme 4 (repeated).

- Introduce the march by emphasizing march rhythm. (Feel it in toes and fingers.)
- For the second listening, emphasize hearing the changes from one part to another.

Development and enrichment alternatives:

1. Tap foot. When music changes, tap fingers, then foot, then fingers.
2. Theme 3 is like a bugle call chord. Sing it.
3. Play theme 3 on bells (C F A C̄).
4. Play a counter melody for theme 3.
5. Let a solo drummer play along with the interlude.
6. Divide the class into four sections. Each section sings (on "ta-ta") or hums one theme.
7. This march is good for formation drills. Plan four patterns, one for each theme. Use interludes for changes.

Related Activities:

Listen to "Stars and Stripes Forever," "Washington Post March," *Chester* by William Schuman (concert or symphonic band), marches for the navy, army, and air force.

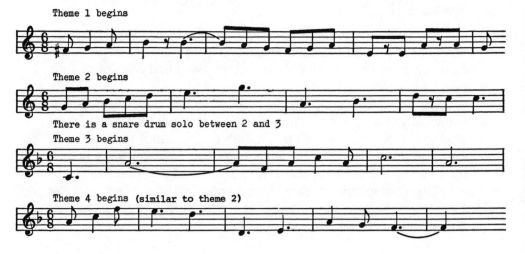

Theme 1 begins

Theme 2 begins

There is a snare drum solo between 2 and 3
Theme 3 begins

Theme 4 begins (similar to theme 2)

CHILDREN'S MARCH
by
Edwin Franko Goldman

Grades: 1 – 3

Focus: Recognizing familiar songs; Moving to march time.

Materials: Recording, Song Source: *Golden Songbook*—Katherine Tyler Wessells. (All songs except "Lazy Mary" and "Four and Twenty Black Birds" are in this book.)

Procedure:

Goldman studied music in New York and played in the Metropolitan Opera Orchestra. However, it was his symphonic band, which he organized in 1912, that made him famous. His best known march is "On the Mall."

In *Children's March,* ten melodies associated with Mother Goose Rhymes are arranged one after another. The songs are:

> Mary Had a Little Lamb
>
> Jingle Bells
>
> Farmer in the Dell
>
> Four and Twenty Black Birds
>
> Lazy Mary
>
> Hickory Dickory Dock
>
> Three Blind Mice
>
> Rock-a-Bye Baby
>
> Pop Goes the Weasel
>
> London Bridge

- Find out how many songs are familiar.
- For the first listening, encourage identifying familiar songs.
- List and sing familiar songs.
- On the second listening, the children may march and sing.

Enrichment:

- Introduce the unfamiliar songs; then repeat the march for the enjoyment of recognition.

- Children select available instruments to play with the recording.
- For solo and group playing encourage children to choose two songs to sing or accompany with instruments when they occur in the piece.

Related Activities:

- Listen to "On the Mall" or use it with a marching formation project.
- Listen to *Mother Goose Songs and Children's Songs,* Reading Readiness Kit, Bowmar-Noble 2178 (Los Angeles).

BUGLES AND DRUMS (1936)
by
Edwin Franko Goldman

Grades: K – 4

Focus: Bugles and Drums; Marching.

Materials: Recording, *March Time,* Mercury 50170; Pictures of bugles and different kinds of drums; Classroom drums.

Procedure:

This excellent march is a "show-off" piece for bugles playing lively tunes on the notes of the tonic chord (do, mi, sol), the natural tones of the bugle, and for the drums elaborating on the basic marching beat. The piece opens with the bugle four times announcing "Here I am" and four times being answered by the symphonic wind ensemble (tutti or all). As the march continues, the bugle and drum continue to dominate.

The drums introduce a bugle solo as the high point of the piece. As the ensemble continues, listen for the diminuendo (gradually getting softer) and the crescendo (gradually getting louder) just before the forceful ending. The piece is in 6/8.

Edwin Franko Goldman organized the American Bandmasters' Association and was its first president. He was interested in music and schools and spent much of his life promoting school music programs.

- Use the first listening to establish a feeling for the march beat.
- Discuss the instruments.
- Study pictures of the bugle and drums.
- Listen again.
- Explore any drums available. Practice a marching beat.
- Explore mouth sounds (ta, ta) for bugle melodies.
- On the third listening, use soft drum beats and mouth sounds to accompany the record.

Enrichment:

- Explore bugle calls of the armed services.
- Use the march as a regular part of the classroom routine, for changing activities, leaving the room, announcing a part of the daily program.

Related Activities:

- Make up your own bugle and drum corps music.
- Listen to the *Children's March* (same recording) and to the *Boy Scouts of America March* (1931)

Piano

LA BAMBOULA

(Opus 2) (For Piano)
by
Louis Moreau Gottschalk

Grades: 3 – 8

Focus: Recognition and reproduction of a basic rhythm and rhythm of a melody.

Materials: Recording, Concord-Disc 1217:217, and/or live performance; Small drum (A second drum or sticks may be useful).

Procedure:

As a child, Gottschalk gave piano and organ concerts and when he was thirteen he was sent to Paris to study music. It was in Paris that he became not only an acclaimed pianist but a composer of music reflecting his New Orleans Creole background and the Negro melodies he had heard as a child. He returned to the United States in 1853 and concertized all over America, from Washington D.C., where he played for President Lincoln, to Nevada and California where he played for the early settlers. He was one of the first American composers to use the elements of Negro music that later evolved into jazz.

- Play excerpts from the piece several times, giving students opportunities to sing the melody and tap the rhythm.
- Play the entire piece. Emphasize listening for the melodies in the excerpts.
- On a second listening, students may tap the basic rhythm pattern or hum (or sing) the melody.
- (Optional) Use a second drum or sticks to tap other rhythms heard in the piece.

Enrichment:

- Plan a dance step to fit the basic rhythmic pattern. All dance to the music. Dance the planned step every time the basic rhythm and theme occur. Individuals dance their own patterns at other times.

- Use different sized drums and other instruments to accompany the music. Divide the instruments into two groups, soft and loud. Soft instruments begin with the rhythm of the melody. Loud instruments play the basic pattern. Practice the two together. Play the recording while the instruments accompany.

Related Activities:

Listen to other pieces by Gottschalk. Pieces he wrote when a young man are "La Savana," "Le Bananier," and "Le Banjo."

TO A WATER LILY
from
Woodland Sketches, Opus 51
by
Edward McDowell

Grades: 1 – 3

Focus: A musical picture; Chordal sounds moving very high and very low.

Materials: *Woodland Sketches,* RCA Victor Basic Record Library for Elementary School—Listening Program Vol. III WE-79; in *Woodland Sketches Selections* VRS 1011 and/or piano score.

Procedure:

Edward McDowell received his musical education in Europe and the romantic tradition of Europe, especially Germany, is reflected in his music. However, he intended his music to be truly American and chose American subjects for his music which he called a "soul-language." He wrote songs, symphonic suites (the most popular being *The Indian Suite*), two piano concertos, and small pieces for piano.

"To a Water Lily" is a sentimental piece—a musical picture of water lilies shifting in a quiet pool or stream.

- To set a quiet mood, use the record or play the piece on the piano.

- To prepare for a second listening, talk about the title of the piece, water lilies, etc.
- Suggest a swaying motion for the children. If it makes the music easier to feel, suggest raising the entire body as the music goes up.
- You may help the children hear the high and low tones better by raising and lowering your hands.
- Alternative: If the children are tired, suggest listening with their heads on the table, eyes closed.

Enrichment:

- For more active listening, some children may stand and indicate the high and low by going up on their toes and crouching on their heels.
- Others may stand and pick up the swaying rhythm.

Related Activities:

Listen to "To a Wild Rose" from the same volume.

JUBA DANCE
(For Piano)
from
In the Bottoms
by
R. Nathaniel Dett

Grades: 3 – 8

Focus: Syncopation; Hand and foot rhythms (active listening).

Materials: Recording, in *Natalie Hinderas Plays Music by Black Composers*, Desto DC-7102A; RCA Victor Basic Record Library for Elementary School—Rhythm Program Vol. VI WE-76.

Procedure:

When Nathaniel Dett was twenty-one, he went to Oberlin, Ohio to study music. Later, he was a long-time director of music at Hampton Institute in Hampton, Virginia. Although he was a concert pianist and a composer of orchestral and choral music, he is most famous for leading choirs and for his collections of spirituals.

A juba is a lively dance from the southern United States. Rhythm is supplied by hand-clapping and foot-tapping, and, sometimes, with the rattle of "the bones," flat sticks about six inches long, shaken between the fingers. Sometimes a fiddler provides the only instrumental accompaniment.

Basic Juba Rhythms

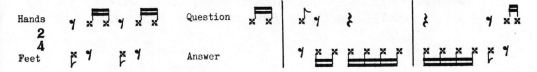

- Introduce the piece as a lively dance.
- Listen to the music.
- Start the 1 – 2 beat with feet.
- Add hands on the weak beats.
- On the second listening, everyone may keep a soft hand and foot rhythm going.
- Work out the question and answer rhythm with hands and feet or with two people (partner clapping).
- On the third listening, let students keep a soft rhythm, changing from the basic beat as they hear it in the music.

Enrichment:

Work out a dance to the music.

Related Activities:

Listen to the entire suite, *In the Bottoms* (Prelude, His Song, Honey, Barcarolle, Juba Dance).

BANSHEE

(about 1923)
by
Henry Cowell

Grades: 3 – 8

Focus: New sounds from the piano.

Materials: Recordings; *Piano Music of Henry Cowell,* Folkways FM 3349; *Tone Cluster Pieces and Other Piano Music,* CRI 109.

Procedure:

Henry Cowell explored all kinds of sounds in his music. He sometimes used familiar instruments in new ways. In this piece describing a Banshee, a female ghost of Irish folk legend, the pianist plays on the strings instead of on the keys. The player stands at the grand piano so he can reach the strings conveniently while an assistant holds the damper pedal down. The mysterious wail of the Banshee is produced by fingers rubbing the strings lengthwise. Other sounds are made by plucking or tapping the strings. The wailing grows louder and louder, then gradually gets softer and softer.

Henry Cowell was one of the first twentieth century American composers to use tone clusters.

- Introduce the record without comment. "What instrument do you hear?" "The piano." "Does it sound like other piano music? Why?"
- Look at the strings of the piano. Demonstrate the sound of fingers strumming the strings (from low to high). Tap fingers on keys. Pluck strings.
- Ask students to identify these techniques in the second listening.
- Lead an exploration in producing new sounds on an autoharp. Strum the strings of the autoharp. Pluck autoharp strings. Tap strings with fingers. Place objects such as pencils, erasers or small pieces of wood on the strings. Strum or tap.
- During the third listening of "Banshee," students show with fingers, hands, arms how the piano is being played.

Enrichment:

- Make up a piece, "New Sounds on the Autoharp."
- Explore making musical sounds on the keyboard while using one, two or three pedals.

Related Activities:

Pianists may play more conventional pieces of Henry Cowell. Two easy ones are "The Irishman Dances," Carl Fischer, and "Bounce Dance," Merion Music.

PRELUDE II
Andante con moto e poco rubato
(Moderate tempo with motion and a little flexibility)
by
George Gershwin

Grades: 4 – 8

Focus: Blues idiom in serious music; The composer, his Americanism.

Materials: Recordings; in *Preludes for Piano,* RCA Victor 2017, in *Piano Pieces – Gershwin,* Folkways 3855; in *Gershwin,* MGM E3307; Keyboard.

Procedure:

As a teenager, George Gershwin studied the piano classics. Then, as he studied music theory, he began to write popular songs in the Tin Pan Alley tradition. He also wrote other kinds of music, a string quartet, a symphonic jazz composition, *Rhapsody in Blue* for piano and orchestra, an opera, *Porgy and Bess,* and the Concerto in F, his most ambitious work. He combined popular and serious music into a new kind of American music.

Prelude II is one of a group of three short preludes for piano. It is sometimes called the "Blue Prelude" because it is a blend of blues-jazz and nineteenth century romantic piano style. It is in A B A form with the first melody in the treble and the second part, a low plaintive tune containing "blue" notes (lowered thirds and sevenths).

- On the first listening, encourage students to remember the first melody. It returns at the end of the piece.
- On a second listening encourage the feeling of the blues rhythm in arms and shoulders.
- The third time, concentrate on the B part. Contrast it with the first part.
- Play the two basic melodies on a keyboard.
- Listen to the piece for the pleasure that understanding gives.

Enrichment:

Move the two melodies to a singing range and put words to them. Emphasize the syncopated rhythm in the words.

Related Activities:

Listen to other Gershwin pieces. *An American In Paris,* an orchestral tone poem, is like a walk through the city with its walking themes and occasional taxi horns. With a map of Paris you may imagine a tour of the city.

LARGO
from
Evocations (Four Chants for Piano)
by
Carl Ruggles

Grades: 4 – 8

Focus: Creative formulae in music; Serial music – a musical chain.

Materials: Recording, Columbia ML – 4986.

Procedure:

When he was a little boy, Carl Ruggles studied violin. As a young man, he studied music at Harvard. Later he went to Winona, Minnesota to found a symphony orchestra. For a long time he lived in a converted schoolhouse in Vermont. He is known as a musical innovator, setting up unusual patterns or musical formulae, then developing them.

In twelve-tone music, no tone may reappear until all eleven other tones have been sounded. In *Evocations,* written in the twelve-tone style, the musical chain is complicated. One of the segments used in "Largo" is actually a combination of two sets of half-step patterns put together.

(1)		F#		G		A♭		A		B♭		B
(2)	C		C#		D		E♭		E		F	

- For the first listening, emphasize the piano performance, tempo of the piece, the irregularity of movement.
- Play and discuss the two half-step patterns. For the second listening, emphasize the movement of the treble, then the bass melodies. Notice the closeness of the notes.
- For the third listening, emphasize how the chain of musical ideas is strung together to make a complete idea.
- Since this kind of music is the opposite of music set in the tonic-dominant tradition, it will seem strange to most people. Listen to it for the freshness and originality of the ideas.

Enrichment:

- Use one of the chromatic rows as a basis for a composition.
- Use the other row for another piece. Later combine the two.

Related Activities:

Listen to the second movement of *Evocations.* The first twelve notes set up a row that is developed into a movement. The movements are:

Largo
Andante con Fantasia
Moderato Appassionato
Adagio Sostenuto

Musical Theater

SHOW BOAT (1927)
and the song
"Ol' Man River"
by
Jerome Kern (Music) and Oscar Hammerstein II (Lyrics)

Grades: 7 – 8

Focus: Musical Comedy Style; "Ol' Man River" — an American favorite.

Materials: Recordings of "Ol' Man River" and/or other songs from *Show Boat.*

Procedure:

The musical comedy, *Show Boat,* was based on a novel of the same name by Edna Ferber. It is a classic not only because of its musical excellence but also because it portrays a chapter of America's past with truth and affection. The real star of the musical is the Mississippi River. (Other songs from the musical are "Make Believe," "Why Do I Love You?", and "Can't Help Lovin' Dat Man.") It is still performed by theatre groups all over the United States. It was made into a film three times.

- Listen to "Ol' Man River"
- Discuss the importance of the Mississippi River to middle America.
- Students sing softly with the recording.

Enrichment:

- Research the story of the musical and the historical facts about river boats.
- Listen to the other songs from the musical.
- Help a group of student singers learn one of the songs.

Related Activities:

Compare the music from *Show Boat* with that of a currently popular musical show.

OKLAHOMA (1943)
by
Richard Rodgers (Music)
and
Oscar Hammerstein II (Lyrics)

Grades: 4 – 8

Focus: Musical Comedy Style; Songs, story, and composer.

Materials: Recording, *Selections from Oklahoma,* MCA 2030 (1973), and/or score for song.

Procedure:

The show *Oklahoma* set off a revival of musical comedy. It became the pattern for musical shows for the next twenty-five years. It is the love story of a cowboy named Curly, and his girl, Laurey, at the time the Oklahoma Territory was admitted to the Union as the forty-sixth state, in 1907.

Curly's opening song, "Oh, What a Beautiful Mornin'" in the cowboy idiom, is a musical description of early morning on the Oklahoma farmlands. "The Surrey with the Fringe on Top" and "People Will Say We're in Love" portray youthful dreams. "Everything's Up to Date In Kansas City" provides a comic interval. The title song, "Oklahoma," sung by the entire cast, brings the story to a climax, celebrating not only the wedding, but Oklahoma as the new state. In the musical comedy tradition, the show moves from dialogue to singing to dancing.

Rodgers has written the music for many shows. He won the Pulitzer prize for *South Pacific.* Some of his other musicals are *Carousel, The King and I,* and *The Sound of Music.*

Hammerstein, who wrote the lyrics, knew the theatre well. His father had been a producer of plays and operas. Earlier in his career he wrote the lyrics for operettas, notably, *Rose Marie* and *Show Boat.*

- Call attention to any current musical comedy and the style. Note the teamwork necessary for composer and lyricist.

- Tell the story and its background.

- Listen to the title song. (This song is performed with a gradual transition from dialogue to singing and on to a dramatic climax with full chorus.)

- On a second listening, encourage students to sing with the recording.

Enrichment:

- Study the early history of Oklahoma.
- Listen to the entire musical, fitting the songs into the story.

Related Activities:

Listen to *South Pacific* and fill in the story.

PUT ON A HAPPY FACE
from
Bye Bye Birdie (1960)
by
Charles Strouse (Music) and Lee Adams (Lyrics)

Grades: 7 – 8

Focus: Musical theatre in 1960.

Materials: Recording of "Put On a Happy Face" or other songs from the musical.

Procedure:

Elvis Presley, "King of Rock" in the fifties, was the inspiration for the musical *Bye Bye Birdie*. It is the story of a rock singer named Conrad Birdie who is leaving for the Army. His fan club of teenage girls compete for the dubious honor of receiving his last kiss before he boards the train. It is a noisy but cheerful and funny musical. Although not as loud, wild or complicated as later musicals, it does contain basic elements of early rock. Songs sung by Conrad are "Honestly Sincere," "One Last Kiss," and "A Lot of Livin' To Do." "Put On a Happy Face" is sung by three sad teenagers at the station. *Bye Bye Birdie* was made into a film in 1963.

- Tell the story of the musical.
- Listen to "Put On a Happy Face."
- Discuss the rhythm of rock music.
- Discuss the music of Elvis Presley.
- Listen to the song again.

Enrichment:

Compare the music of *Bye Bye Birdie* with currently popular songs.

Related Activities:

Attend a performance of a musical.

MARCH OF THE THREE KINGS

Suite from *Amahl and the Night Visitors* (1951)
by
Gian-Carlo Menotti

Grades: 1 – 6

Focus: The story; Drama, dance and music.

Materials: Recording, *Suite-Introduction, March of the Three Kings, Dance of the Shepherds* in "Stories in Ballet and Opera" Bowmar-Noble 071; Opera – RCA Victor LM 2762; LSC 2762.

Procedure:

Menotti came to the United States in 1928 when he was seventeen. He studied music at the Curtis Institute in Philadelphia. He is one of the most prolific American composers of opera. In addition to *Amahl and the Night Visitors,* he wrote *The Old Maid and the Thief* (1939), *The Medium* (1946), and *The Consul* (1950). His music is a combination of traditional Romantic harmonies and melodies and contemporary irregular rhythms and dissonant harmonies—a kind of fusing of the old and the new.

Amahl and the Night Visitors is a short opera often performed during the Christmas season. It was the first opera written especially for television. A boy soprano sings the role of Amahl.

The story begins with Amahl, a crippled shepherd boy sitting outside his desert hut, watching a brilliant star and playing his shepherd's pipes. Three kings, on their way to see the Christ Child, stop for the night. Neighboring shepherds come to pay homage and dance for the kings. The climax comes at the end when Amahl offers his crutch as a gift to the Christ Child and is cured. He goes with the kings to Bethlehem, carrying his crutch as a gift.

The Suite has three parts; the Introduction which is quiet and flowing, the "March of the Three Kings," and the "Dance of the Shepherds." The oboe sounds like a shepherd's pipe.

The March of the Three Kings

- Tell the story. How would the kings march? How would they be dressed? What does a night sky over the desert look like? How do you picture Amahl? The hut? His mother?
- Listen to the Introduction and the "March of the Three Kings."
- Plan a march.
- On the second listening, children may march like kings.
- Plan parts for small instruments like a drum, sticks, a tambourine, jingle sticks.
- On the next listening, some may march, others play instruments.

Enrichment:

Make simple costumes for the dramatization (paper crowns for the kings, scarves or coats for capes, a tree branch for a crutch, a paper apron for the mother.

Related Activities:

Listen to a recording of the Vienna Boys Choir, or to other records of children's voices. This establishes a standard of singing quality.

The Symphony Orchestra

A symphony orchestra is made up of about one hundred instruments divided into four groups or families: strings—violins, violas, cellos, double basses, harps; woodwinds—piccolos, flutes, oboes, English horns, clarinets, bassoons; brasses—trumpets, trombones, French horns, tubas; percussion—tympani, bass and snare drums, celesta, xylophone, tambourine, triangle, cymbals, and sometimes, instruments for special sound effects. Any other instrument scored by the composer is added.

A conductor follows the master score, and, by means of his hands, body motions, facial expressions, and usually, a baton, directs and unifies the playing to produce the performance intended by the composer.

THE SYMPHONY

A symphony is a large composition for orchestra and is usually in four movements, like four related pieces. In form it is somewhat like a sonata for piano or other solo instrument. Each movement has at least two themes, a primary one and secondary one. The composer uses the orchestral instruments in his own way to create a musical composition.

The first movement of *The Children's Symphony* by Harl McDonald (1899–1955) is used for this study. *The Children's Symphony* is a straightforward, easy-to-understand composition with melodies of familiar English nursery rhymes used as themes. (These nursery rhymes were first published in England in 1760 as "Mother Goose's Melody.") These melodies have been sung by American children for about two hundred years. Hearing these familiar tunes will help the children identify the structure of the music and the devices the composer uses to develop a symphony.

CHILDREN'S SYMPHONY, FIRST MOVEMENT

by Harl McDonald

Grades: 2 – 8

Focus: Understanding a symphony movement (4–8); Recognition of familiar tunes (2–4); Recognition of percussion instruments used in the connecting parts.

Materials: 1. Recording, Adventures in Music Record Library — RCA, Grade 3, vol. 2.

2. Chalk and chalkboard or felt pen and chart paper (4–8); or cutouts of bridge and sheep and flannelboard (2–3).

3. Pictures of percussion instruments (snare and bass drum, tympani, and cymbals).

Procedure:

The first movement of a symphony is cheerful and lively, and historically, is in sonata form which is an elaborate ternary or A B A form. This movement is marked allegro moderato (moderately lively). The primary theme is "London Bridge." The secondary theme is "Baa, Baa, Black Sheep" ("Twinkle, Twinkle, Little Star" or "Ah! vous, dirai-je, Maman").

After a short introduction, the first section (A) begins with the primary theme which is repeated in full and in part during this section. A percussion interlude connects section A with section B when the second theme is played. After section B, the percussion instruments introduce the A section again. At the end there is a short coda (an added ending).

The composer makes changes in the melodies, uses fragments, changes keys and modes (major or minor) and combines different instruments to develop the themes and make the composition interesting.

(If the children are already familiar with the tunes used as themes, skip steps 1 and 2).

- Sing and/or play "London Bridge" until it is familiar.
- Sing and/or play "Baa, Baa, Black Sheep" until it is familiar.
- Review the melodies.

- Listen for the tunes as the record is played. (Which is played first? second? last?)
- (Grades 2, 3) Listen once more and put the song cutouts on the flannelboard as the songs are introduced.
- (Grades 4–8) Plot the form on the chalkboard or paper (Introduction, A, Percussion Interlude, B, Percussion Interlude, A, Coda).

Enrichment:

- (Grades 2–3) Sing the songs as you hear them.
- Listen for the bass and snare drums, and cymbals.
- (Grades 4–8) Identify the instruments playing the themes and interludes.
- Create a short dance for each theme. Dance with the music.

Related Activities:

- (Grades 2, 3) Play the game for "London Bridge."
- (Grades 4–8) Listen to Mozart's "Variations on 'Ah! vous dirai-je, Maman'" for piano.

How to play "London Bridge"

Two players stand opposite each other, joining hands and forming a bridge. Children pass under the bridge as all sing. When the words, "My fair lady" are sung, the bridge keepers drop their arms and catch the child passing through. He is asked (in a whisper) "Do you like gold or silver?" (The keepers have already chosen one or the other.) The child stands behind the "silver" or "gold." After all the children are caught, the game ends with a tug of war. Some traditional verses are:

> London Bridge is falling down, my fair lady.
> Build it up with iron bars, etc.
> Iron bars will bend and break, etc.
> Build it up with pins and needles, etc.
> Pins and needles rust and bend, etc.
> Build it up with gold and silver, etc.
> Gold and silver I've not got, etc.

Children add their own verses.

MERRY MOUNT SUITE

by
Howard Hanson

Grades: 4 – 8

Focus: "Color" in the orchestra.

Materials: 1. Recording, *The Composer and His Orchestra,* Mercury MG 50175.
2. Instruments of the Orchestra Charts, Bowmar-Noble Company.

Procedure:

A composer uses the instruments of the orchestra to produce the effects or to "paint the colors" he wants. In most large symphonic compositions the composer uses all the choirs—strings, woodwinds, brasses, and percussion.

In this recording, Howard Hanson analyzes his *Merry Mount Suite* and shows how he "mixed" the sounds or "colors" of the instruments.

This is a great opportunity for children to hear each instrument of the orchestra alone and with other instruments in the same choir, and different choirs blended to help the composer produce his musical idea. After all the instruments and combinations are demonstrated, the entire piece is played ("Overture," "Children's Dance," "Maypole Dances").

- Explain the purpose of the recording. Show pictures of the orchestral instruments.

- Listen to the sections as many times as students want to hear them. If interest in individual instruments is high, extend the lessons into a unit. Sections need not be listened to in sequence. The development of aural identification of instrumental "color" varies from one student to another. The recording may be made available at a listening post.

- Periodically, throughout a series of lessons, play the last part of the recording that has the entire piece. Students will be interested in how many instruments, as well as motifs, phrases, and sections they recognize.

Enrichment:

Ask students who are studying orchestral instruments to demonstrate their instruments. Have them show how the instrument is put together, how it is held, and how it is played—the range, different kinds of sounds, etc.

Related Activities:

- Relate this study to Harl McDonald's *Children's Symphony*
- Listen to a symphony concert on television, or at a concert hall.

HUMOR

from the *Afro-American Symphony*
by
William Grant Still

Grades: 6 – 8

Focus: Blues elements and the banjo in the symphony orchestra

Materials: Recording of Third Movement, *Afro American Symphony*, Victor Records 2059-B; Preservation of American Musical Heritage, MOA 118.

Procedure:

William Grant Still was ethnically a fusion of Europe, Africa, and North America. His father was Scottish, Negro, Indian; his mother was Negro, Indian, Spanish and Irish. In addition, he had experience with Creole music and he learned about Hebraic music when he was commissioned to compose for a New York synagogue. In the *Afro-American Symphony* he used the Negro idiom as a core, then branched out into all the ethnic strains of his background. He was one of the first twentieth century avant-garde American composers. (His music was experimental and "different" from the general feeling of the times.)

The symphony is in four parts—Longing (moderato assai), Sorrow (Adagio), Humor (animato), Aspiration (Lento, con risoluzione). Each part is introduced with a poem by Paul Laurence Dunbar.

The symphony uses the blues scale (example: C D E♭ F G A B♭ B). Although the harmonies are basically conventional triads, he adds sixths, sevenths, and ninths for color. Another unique feature is his use of the banjo as a symphonic instrument.

The third movement of most symphonies is a dance-like movement or a scherzo, light playful music. This contrasts with the generally slow second movement.

A general outline of the movement is:

1. Development of principal theme by the woodwinds and strings, then brasses and low strings.
2. Banjo used intermittently
3. Strings and woodwinds carry the melodic line just before coda. Blues scale (in A♭) played by trumpets and trombones.
4. Full orchestra.

• Spend some time on the background of the composer, emphasizing the meaning of avant-garde.
• Listen to the music, focusing on why he called it "Humor."
• Discuss the general pattern of instrumental use and when to listen for the banjo.
• Explain the blues scale.
• Listen again. Try to hear the beginning of the coda.
• Discuss the music as a complete composition.

Enrichment:

• Arrange a banjo demonstration.
• Play the blues scale in even rhythm. After several playings, play it using a long-short rhythmic pattern. Encourage improvisation.

Related Activities:

Listen to other music by W. G. Still:

• *Three Visions* (piano), Desto no. D.C.-7102.
• Suite for Violin and Piano, Folk music of North America, Orion ORS 7152 (Los Angeles).

Program Music

Program music is focused on a central idea which may not be a musical idea but is expressed in music. The idea may be pictorial, fictional, or expressive of definite feelings. The title of the composition gives the performer and listener a clue to the central idea and the general nature of the composition.

CHESTER
from
New England Triptych for Orchestra (1956)
by
William Schuman

Grades: 4 – 8

Focus: "Chester," a heritage song in a contemporary setting.

Materials: Recording, RCA LSC-3060;

Key words: augmented – enlarged, slowed
diminished – shortened
triptych – a set of three pictures, in this
case musical pictures

Procedure:

William Schuman is primarily a symphonist but has also written choral works, a one act baseball opera, *The Mighty Casey,* and music for ballet. At one time he was president of the Juilliard School of Music and, in 1962, was appointed president of the Lincoln Center for the Performing Arts in New York.

The *New England Triptych* develops three choral works of William Billings into an orchestral work. The tunes are "Be Glad, Then, America," "When Jesus Wept," and in the final section, "Chester," the hymn tune that became the marching song of the Continental Army.

In this piece "Chester" is first played as a hymn. Then the woodwinds play it much faster, the brass join the woodwinds to play it much slower (augmented). Later, the trumpet and strings play it shortened (diminished) and then as a hymn. Schuman gives all parts of the orchestra an opportunity to play at least fragments of the hymn tune.

- Review the song "Chester" and its history until it is familiar. Singing or humming it will help students remember it.
- On the first listening, help students recognize the song.
- On the second listening, encourage recognition of song fragments.
- On the third listening, emphasize the recognition of instruments playing the hymn. Also, bring out how the composer has used a composed song but has made the piece his own.

Enrichment:

- Use "Chester," or an easier song like "Old Brass Wagon" as the basis for a class composition. Divide available instruments into sections (voices, bells, keyboard, recorder, autoharp and guitar, percussion). Use all or part of the song, all or some of the instruments in your own way.
- Listen to the other two movements of the triptych.

Related Activities:

- Listen to *Chester* (1957) for concert band written by the same composer (Columbia ML – 5496; Mer-Dec 8633: 78633).
- Listen to *William Billings' Overture* (1943) by the same composer.
- Listen to "Chester" as played on a restored organ (1827), (Columbia ML 5496).

FATHER OF WATERS
from
The Mississippi Suite
by
Ferde Grofé

Grades: 4 – 6

Focus: Musical Description – Program Music, describing a place or event or suggesting a mood.

Materials: *Mississippi Suite,* Columbia ML 2046; Bells or keyboard or other melody instrument.

Procedure:

As a child, Ferde Grofé was surrounded by musicians. His grandfather was a cellist; his uncle was concertmaster for the Los Angeles Symphony; his father was a singer. He studied music theory with his mother.

For a while he played the viola in the Los Angeles Symphony. Then he went into the business world and back to music again, playing one of his three major instruments, violin, viola or piano. In 1920, he started playing with Paul Whiteman's orchestra and later became the arranger. He first became famous for his orchestral arrangement of Gershwin's *Rhapsody in Blue* (1924).

The *Mississippi Suite* is one of several suites he wrote, the most famous being *The Grand Canyon Suite*. The four sections of *The Mississippi Suite* are "Father of Waters," "Huckleberry Finn," "Old Creole Days," and "Mardi Gras."

In the first section, Grofé describes the mighty river as the "Father of Waters" and uses as his main theme a broad, powerful four-tone melody introduced by the brasses. Rippling water is suggested by the strings in the background. Scales and rhythms suggestive of Indian music appear throughout.

- Talk about the magnitude of the river, the industries and people along its banks, its power, potentially destructive forces, and how the river affects the lives of thousands of people.
- For the first listening, present the music as a tribute to the river.
- Before the second listening, describe the River theme—a slow melody in the key of C minor hovering around middle C.
- Also suggest listening for the tremolo of the strings. Encourage original ideas that the music might suggest.
- After the second listening, discuss the piece as program music.

Enrichment:

1. At another time, listen for instrumentation, melodies, rhythms.
2. Relate the piece to the study of early explorers—De Soto, La Salle, Joliet, Marquette.

Related Activities:

1. Listen to the second section and relate it to Mark Twain's hero, Huckleberry Finn.
2. Present the last two sections as mood and carnival music.

Variations

VARIATIONS ON AMERICA
by
Charles Ives

Grades: 1 – 8

Focus: Variations as a form in music; Youth involvement in music.

Materials: Recording, in *The Organ in America,* E. Power Biggs, Organist, Columbia ML 5496; RCA LSC 2893; in *Charles Ives; The 100th Anniversary,* Columbia M4 32504.

Procedure:

Ives improvised these variations at a Fourth of July recital in 1891 when he was sixteen years old. The variations reflect the fun and excitement of an old-time Fourth of July program. They were certainly not intended for anything more than an expression of the happiness and significance of the day. Ives is quoted as saying that playing the pedals in the last variation was almost as much fun as playing baseball.

Improvisation—the composing of music as you play it—is very creative. Students who have a good understanding of their instrument and the basic fundamentals of music are more apt to be successful improvisors.

- Introduce the record as the work of a sixteen year old.
- Suggest listening for the familiar melody.
- Before the second listening, talk about the ways a melody may be varied. Outline the composition and suggest finding the beginning of each variation. Discuss the organ as a versatile instrument.
- The third listening is for the enjoyment of the music as a part of an Independence Day celebration.

Enrichment:

- Make a class variation on *America.* Use bells or keyboard for melody, autoharp or guitar for chords, percussion for rhythms. Play it as sung. Then change it in some of these ways—play it twice as fast; twice as slow; play it as a march; change strums on autoharp or guitar; play it higher or lower; percussion instruments improvise a fancy rhythm pattern.

• For a field trip, arrange a demonstration on a pipe organ.

Related Activities:

• Listen to other American compositions played on historic organs. (Same recording.)
• Listen to *New England Holidays* (Washington's Birthday, Decoration Day, Fourth of July, Thanksgiving) (1904–1913), CRI 190.

AMERICAN SALUTE (1943)
by
Morton Gould

Grades: 1 – 8

Focus: (Grades 1 – 3) Marching song; (Grades 4 – 8) Theme and variation in orchestral music; Familiar song as a theme.

Materials: Recording in *Music of Morton Gould,* Columbia ML 54218; Grades 1 – 3, Kazoos, hummers, or combs with paper, drums; Grades 4 – 8, Bells and autoharp; Music for "When Johnny Comes Marching Home" (generally included in traditional song collections).

Procedure:

Morton Gould was an exceptional child musician, able to play by ear, compose pieces, and improvise on a melody in recital. As a teenager, he studied at New York University for two years. As a young man, he earned his living playing the piano in vaudeville, making recordings, and giving illustrated lectures. Later, he conducted, composed and arranged music for orchestral radio programs. He also composed for the theater and for symphonic band.

In the *American Salute* he uses the popular song "When Johnny Comes Marching Home" as the theme, fusing popular and classical structures, as a theme and variations. Just before World War II, he conducted government-sponsored programs that included pieces characterizing allied countries. He wrote this piece to represent the United States.

"When Johnny Comes Marching Home" was composed in 1863, the year of the Emancipation Proclamation. After the Civil War was over, bands often played the song at Peace Jubilees. It was also popular during the Spanish-American War in 1898. The song is in the Aeolian mode or natural minor.

- Play the melody of the march song, "When Johnny Comes Marching Home" on a keyboard, bells, or any chromatic instrument. Emphasize the marching rhythm.
- Hum, clap, tap, step or in some other way fix the melody and rhythm in mind.
- Listen to the recording and identify the song. (It occurs first after the introduction.) Listen for bassoon, snare drum, violins.

Grades 1– 3

- On a second listening, let the children play kazoos or sing the melody as they recognize it.
- On another listening, add drums playing soft accompaniment. (Children will have to listen for changes.)
- As the drums play with the recording, the other children follow the leader in a marching parade.

Grades 4–8

- After an interlude featuring the snare drum, listen for the main theme played by oboes and English horn and accompanied by bass clarinet and bassoon.
- Listen for the main theme played by strings and the interlude with brass, tympani, and snare drum.
- After two more careful listenings, discuss the instrumentation as it varies the piece, the entrances of the theme and the interludes.
- Discuss how the piece presents a musical theme, then varies it by changing the key, tempo, register, dynamics, or by using only part of the theme. (There are three variations after the main theme is introduced. They are separated by interludes.)

The piece ends with the orchestra playing the theme in unison. Find these things in the music. (If time is limited, use this for a second lesson.)

• Play the theme on bells with chords on autoharp or guitar.

Enrichment:

(Grades 4 – 8) Sing other songs of the Civil War period—"Battle Hymn of the Republic," "Tramp, Tramp, Tramp."

Related Activities:

Listen to other compositions by Morton Gould—*Cowboy Rhapsody* or *Lincoln Legend*.

Music for Film

DREAM MARCH AND CIRCUS MUSIC
from
The Red Pony
by
Aaron Copland

Grades: 1 – 4

Focus: Like and unlike music; Music describing a scene.

Materials: Recording, Decca DL 9616.

Procedure:

Aaron Copland studied music while he was growing up, then went to France to study. In 1924, he returned to the United States determined to write music that would be very American. He wrote music for radio and films, an opera, ballets, music for speaker and orchestra, and symphonic suites like this one based on his film music for *The Red Pony*. It is for a small orchestra with woodwinds, brass and percussion instruments predominating.

There are six parts to the suite:

Morning on the Ranch

The Gift (the pony)

Dream March and Circus Music

Walk to the Bunkhouse

Grandfather's Story

Happy Ending (much like part one)

The story is about a boy named Jody who, with his father, mother, grandfather and a cowboy named Billy Buck, lived on a ranch in California. One day Jody's father gave him a red pony. Billy Buck gave him a red leather saddle and taught him how to care for the pony that Jody named Gabilan (hawk).

In the "Dream March," Jody dreams that he and Billy Buck are knights in silver armor.

The "Circus Music" begins with loud chords that could be the entrance and taking a bow. Then, there is prancing music and an imitation of a calliope. Jody dreams he is the ringmaster.

- Lead a discussion of the children's experiences at a circus. Use pictures to help those without experience.
- Make a list of things seen and heard at a circus.
- Emphasize these things for the first listening.
- Discuss what the children heard in the music.
- For the second listening, emphasize the contrasting parts and the imagined scene.

Enrichment:

Experiment on keyboard or bells to make the dissonant sounds of a calliope. Play a group of three black keys (or bars) as a block of sound. Contrast this with a group of three white keys (or bars). Try F G A, G A B, C D E. Combine the chosen sounds into a calliope sound.

ACADIAN SONGS AND DANCES

from
Louisiana Story (1948)
by
Virgil Thompson

Grades: 4 – 8

Focus: Music for films; Contrasting movements in a suite.

Materials: Recording, Epic LC-3809; BC-1147; Chalkboard or chart; Pencil and paper for each student.

Procedure:

Virgil Thompson, like Aaron Copland and other American composers, used folk melodies in his music. In this suite, a concert piece which he arranged from his score for the film, *Louisiana Story,* he uses seven songs of the Cajun river people, descendants of the French settlers who migrated from Acadia in Nova Scotia to Louisiana. Each of the songs is the basis of a movement or section. They are "Sadness," "Papa's Tune," "A Narrative," "The Alligator and the 'Coon," "Super-Sadness," "Walking Song," "The Squeeze Box."

Although very important for determining mood and describing an incident, background music for a film is generally not listened to as music. When this music is arranged as a concert piece, it becomes the center of attention.

Up to the time of Bach a suite was a series of dances. The modern suite may be a series of dances or a free succession of contrasting movements.

Alternate Procedures

One

- Introduce the music as a seven-movement suite without titles. During the first listening have students write a one-or two-word descriptive title for each movement. (Each student should have a paper with numbers 1 to 7 down the left margin of the page.) If necessary, repeat a movement.
- A comparison of titles will be interesting to everyone. A review of each movement to explain why certain titles were chosen will focus attention on the music.
- After another listening, students may collaborate on titles or keep their own.

Two

- Put names of movements on the board or chart.
- Keep track of each change during the first listening.
- For the second listening, select one movement for careful attention.
- Discuss the appropriateness of the title, instrumentation, form (A B A, etc.), rhythm, melody, harmonies.
- Give the selected movement a third listening for full understanding.

Enrichment:

- Use the movements "Sadness" and "Super-Sadness." Make them a study of mood. Put emphasis on the reasons for one being "super-sad."
- Use movements six and seven as the basis for a free or patterned dance.

Related Activities:

To explore other film scores of Virgil Thompson, listen to *The Plow That Broke the Plains* (1936), or *The River* (1937).

WALKING SONG AND THE SQUEEZE BOX

from
Acadian Songs and Dances
by
Virgil Thompson

Grades: 1 – 3

Focus: Creative Movement.

Materials: Recording, Epic LC-3809; BC-1147; Floor space—extended arm's length for each child.

Procedure:

- Before the first listening, explain that there are two parts.
- Have children listen for the change: (walking, duple rhythm, second part, triple rhythm).
- Discuss and explore the kinds of movement for each part.
- During a second listening have children walk from their seats to the free space, extending arms to establish dance territory.
- When "The Squeeze Box" begins, each child moves to the rhythm in his own way. (If the teacher is leading, demonstrating, or suggesting movements, start with the whole body swaying, then the upper torso and head, then feet to waist, one foot, two feet, one arm, two arms, and gradually back to the whole body.
- Repeat "Walking Song" to get the children back to their seats. This makes an A B A form.

Enrichment:

- At subsequent listening and dance sessions, children may move in one direction around the room, gradually changing places.

- For more movement, small groups may take turns, leaving more space for large, free movements.

Related Activities:

For a quiet listening period, the whole suite may be played with the last two movements being the "wake up" time.

Chamber Music

ALLEGRO
(First Movement)
Trio in A Minor, Opus 150
(1939)
by
Amy Beach (Mrs. H. H. A.)

Grades: 4 – 8; 1 – 3 for background listening.

Focus: Musical Sounds of a Trio (Piano, violin, cello).

Materials: Recording, in *Contemporary American Chamber Music,*
Dorian Records LP 1007.

Procedure:

When Amy Cheney (Beach) was four years old, she composed a piece in her head and called it "Snowflake Waltz." Then, she went inside and played it on the piano. She loved to play the piano and taught herself many things about music by analyzing the pieces she studied.

When she grew up, she not only concertized all over the United States and Europe, she also wrote many songs, a piano concerto, some chamber music, anthems and a mass, and piano pieces for children.

In this trio, the piano, cello and violin are of equal importance. The piano sets the stage with a rippling accompaniment over which the cello states the first theme; the violin repeats it; then they all join in together.

The second theme is a kind of song introduced by the violin. The three instruments weave patterns of sound with the theme material. The movement ends with a feeling of majesty—perhaps of triumph, with piano chords supporting string melodies.

- To introduce the piece, suggest listening for each instrument as it enters.
- Listen to the first part that ends just before the violin plays the second theme.
- Discuss the entrances, the melodies, solos and accompaniment, the blend of sounds and the instruments.

- On the second listening, the organization of the piece will begin to be more evident. Point out the beginning of the second part.
- After the second listening, talk about the ending, how it differs from the beginning and how it provides a climax for the piece.
- Listen a third time.

This is a particularly good example of the blends of a trio. The individual solos at the beginning give the student an opportunity to hear the music build into combined harmony.

Enrichment:

- Listen to the second movement, "Lento espressivo and Presto." This movement is a good example of a slow moving part followed by a very fast part.
- Listen to the third movement, "Allegro con brio." This movement contains some of the same melodic elements as the first movement. It is a happy ending.

SUITE FOR WIND QUINTET
by
Ruth Crawford Seeger

Grades: 6 – 8

Focus: Blending sounds of wind instruments (clarinet, flute, oboe, horn, bassoon); Movements of a suite.

Materials: Recording, Composers Recording Inc., SD 249; *Meet the Instruments Posters,* no. 123, Bowmar-Noble.

Procedure:

This suite was the last composition written by Ruth Crawford Seeger. It reflects changes in her composition toward more complicated counterpoint and rhythms.

In this piece, the student will have an opportunity to hear each instrument playing a major part while being supported by the other instruments as well as in ensemble. In the first movement, there is an interesting section where the instruments play in unison, then move back to the dissonant harmonies. The clarinet introduces the slow second movement, then the other instruments take their turns alone and together. The rhythm is very flexible and is not the kind of music students will tap with their feet.

The French horn is used in many different instrumental combinations because it seems to blend with and complement any sounds with which it is combined.

- Discuss the reed instruments (clarinet, oboe, and bassoon), the transverse flute, and the horn. Use pictures.
- Listen to the piece, identifying the three movements and as many instruments as possible.
- Discuss the things the students noticed about the music.
- Next, listen for unison playing in the first movement, the clarinet introduction in the second movement, the jolly bassoon, flute and the other instruments joining them in the last movement. Use these as landmarks and to direct students in their own kind of listening.
- Discuss the music once more, allowing for student impressions.

Enrichment:

A live demonstration of any of the instruments will enhance further listening.

Electronic Music

All music is some kind of controlled sound projecting a musical idea. Pitch, duration, and texture, in simple or complex arrangements, are the basic elements. In this respect, electronic music is no different from other music.

However, electronic music goes beyond the boundaries of traditional music. It is produced by electronic tape, a synthesizer capable of producing innumerable sounds, or a computer. Raw materials may be natural sounds modified and transformed into electrical signals or they may be sounds generated directly in the form of electrical waves. In an electronic music studio, three operations produce a composition: (1) The signals or sounds are generated; (2) These sounds are modified; (3) Individual and groups of sounds are organized into a finished composition.

A synthesizer is somewhat like a super organ. It consists of a keyboard and a panel of jacks that are connected by patch cords in different combinations and programmed to suit the composer. In addition, large synthesizers have a sequencer that programs repeated patterns. Small synthesizers are generally pre-programmed.

A PIECE FOR TAPE RECORDER (1956)
by
Vladimir Ussachevsky

Grades: 6 – 8

Focus: Manipulating instrumental and natural sounds.

Materials: Recording, Composers Recordings Inc., 112.

Procedure:

Ussachevsky came to the United States when he was nine years old. He studied music at the Eastman School of Music and at Columbia University. In 1959, He became one of the directors of the Columbia-Princeton Electronic Music Center in New York.

The structure of this piece is a gradual transition from recognizable musical sounds to a complex spectrum of unrecognizable sounds. Raw materials consisted of non-electronic sounds—a gong, a piano, a cymbal, tympani, chords on an organ, and the noise of a jet plane. Electronic sounds were pure tones produced on an oscillator and a tremolo produced by reverberation of a click from a tape recorder switch.

- Present the piece as a change from natural to manipulated sounds.
- Identify sounds from the beginning of the piece.
- On a second listening, point out how the sounds are sequenced and when they begin to be distorted. Ask for opinions as to the climax of the piece.

Enrichment:

- Listen to *Lemon Drops* by Kenneth Gaburo, Heliodor H S 25047.
- For more sophisticated listening use *Rhapsodic Variations for Tape Recorder and Orchestra,* Louisville 545-5; works by Ibert and Read.

COMPOSITION FOR SYNTHESIZER
by
Milton Babbitt

Grades: 6 – 8

Focus: Sounds of the synthesizer.

Materials: Recording, Columbia MS — 6566; Folkways FM 3704.

Procedure:

Milton Babbitt was raised in Jackson, Mississippi. At New York University he studied mathematics and later, music. He began teaching at Princeton University in 1938. In 1959 he became one of the four directors of the Columbia-Princeton Electronic Music Center in New York. He wrote serial music before he began his experiments in electronic music.

The *Composition for Synthesizer* was created on the RCA Electronic Sound Synthesizer at Columbia University. All the sounds and transformations were created on the synthesizer at Mr. Babbitt's dictation.

- Introduce the piece by reviewing the characteristics of a synthesizer. Emphasize that electronic sounds are different from and of greater variety and range than traditional instrumental sounds.
- For the first listening, suggest listening for a variety of sounds.
- On the second listening, suggest listening for one or more of the following—pitches, tone colors, rhythms (even or uneven or none at all), dynamics, density of sound.
- On the third listening, suggest listening for repetitions, definite breaks or contrasts that might give the piece form.

Enrichment:

At another listening, use these graphic markings to plot the music—lines for melodies, dots for explosive sounds, multiple lines for melodies moving together, geometric figures to block textures.

Related Activities:

Listen to *Nonesuch Guide to Electronic Music* by Paul Beaver and Bernard Krause, Nonesuch HC - 73018.

ARIA WITH FONTANA MIX (1958)
by
John Cage

Grades: 6 – 8

Focus: Chance electronic music.

Materials: Recordings; There are several versions — Time S 8003 and Mainstream MS - 5005; Time 58003; *Fontana Mix* in Electronics and Percussion - Five Realizations by Max Neuhaus (Columbia MS 7139).

Procedure:

John Cage is generally said to be the inventor of chance or aleatory music. This twentieth century device results in music without the organization, or plan, that most other music has. Controlled chance provides some framework. The composer may supply the notes and leave their order to the performer; he may stipulate the time allowed for improvisation, direct the performer to begin the piece where his eyes fall, provide alternatives throughout the piece, or, in the case of an ensemble, let individual performers begin improvisation at random.

The *Fontana Mix* is a wild collection of electronic, environmental, and musical sounds spliced together in quick and unrelated succession. The aria is a vocal improvisation using different singing styles. With this combination, a complex array of sounds results.

- On the first listening, ask the students to determine what the composer intended—a series of sounds, a piece directed toward a climax, or a piece to establish a mood.
- On the second listening, students may be able to identify, or at least isolate, different sounds.
- On the third listening, students may be able to picture the sequences of the piece with descriptive lines, dots, or geometrics.

Enrichment:

Using mouth, hand or foot sounds, or available instruments, let each student add a short phrase to a "sound chain."

Related Activities:

Tape a sound chain made by the class.

PART FOUR

Moving with American Music

GALLOPING AND SKIPPING

Sally Go Round
Pop! Goes the Weasel

FROM BASIC MOVEMENTS TO SINGING GAMES

Toodala
Hey Betty Martin
One Day One Foot Kept Moving
Bluebird

MOVEMENT AND MOOD

All the Pretty Little Horses
Chicken Reel

INDIAN MUSIC

Moccasin Song
Navajo Happy Song

CREATIVITY AND IMAGINATION

Syncopated Clock
On the Fourth of July
Goodbye Old Paint

PLAY PARTY DANCES

Love Somebody
Old Brass Wagon
Sourwood Mountain

ROUNDS FOR DANCING

Row, Row, Row Your Boat
Where Is John?

PATTERNED MOVEMENT

The Sidewalks of New York
Stars and Stripes Forever
Simple Gifts
Hawaiian Boat Song

Galloping and Skipping

SALLY GO ROUND
(Sonny Go Round)

Grades: K – 1

Focus: Galloping; feeling a long-short rhythmic pattern.

Materials: Ample floor space.

Procedure:

Singing about the impossible has always been a delight to children. In this old singing game, the stars and moon seem just as accessible as the chimney pot.

- Sing the song, emphasizing the long-short pattern.
- Sing together and clap the rhythm.
- Ask for a volunteer to gallop or move to the rhythm.
- All the children gallop through the song one time.
- Plan the position of the stars, moon, and the chimney pot. Use chairs or tape on the floor for markers. Three children may hold pictures and stand for the three positions.
- Plan a traffic pattern around the stars, moon and chimney pot.
- Play a follow-the-leader game along the traffic pattern. If the class is too large, a few children at a time may travel.
- Children take turns being the leader.

Enrichment:

Verse for galloping around the room.

> Gallop around the room, Gallop around the room;
> Gallop and gallop gallop and gallop and
> Gallop around the room.

Related Activities:

The good gallopers may be ready to skip. You may use this song to introduce skipping.

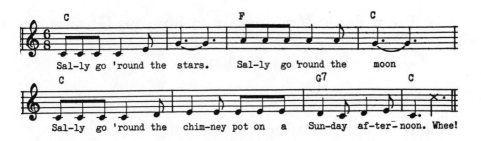

Sal-ly go 'round the stars. Sal-ly go 'round the moon
Sal-ly go 'round the chim-ney pot on a Sun-day af-ter-noon. Whee!

POP! GOES THE WEASEL

Grades: K – 1

Focus: Skipping.

Materials: (Optional) Melody Instrument when used without singing; score (in most school texts).

Procedure:

- Talk about skipping, "First one foot, then the other."
- Ask for volunteers. (Check to determine whether the children gallop or skip.)
- As the demonstrator skips, start the music, adapting the tempo to that of the demonstrator.
- To help a child who wants to skip but can't, hold his hand and skip with him.
- Play the entire piece. The "pop" may be used for a broad jump and a place to stop.

From Basic Movements to Singing Games

TOODALA

Grades: K – 2

Focus: Variations on basic movements (walk, run, jump, hop).

Materials: Ample floor space.

Procedure:

This old "dance song" lends itself well to reviewing the basic movements, then varying them. The beginning words imply individual participation that can easily be developed into group activities.

- All sit in a circle around the room.
- Sing and clap the song.
- Ask one child to walk as you clap the rhythm.
- Start the singing while the child continues.
- Everyone copies the demonstrated walk as the song is repeated.
- Ask for volunteers to do another kind of walk. (If necessary, suggest animals, a clown, or a mood walk—happy or sad.) Everyone copies the walk and sings.
- The lesson may continue using only variations of walks or it may move into variations of run, jump, and hop, depending on time and interest.

Toodala

Play Party Game from Texas

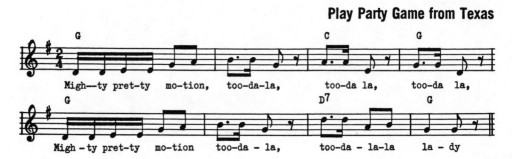

Migh—ty pret-ty mo-tion, too-da-la,   too-da la,   too-da la,

Migh—ty pret-ty mo-tion too-da-la,   too-da-la-la   la-dy

Enrichment:

Choose a timely subject and limit the verses to that subject, perhaps a holiday or a season.

HEY BETTY MARTIN

Grades: K – 2

Focus: Foot movements in rhythm (tiptoe in duple time).

Materials: Ample Floor space.

Procedure:

This song dates back to 1800. It probably originated in New England, and was later brought to the midwest.

- Sing the song with strong accents.
- Ask one child to demonstrate walking on tiptoe.
- Everyone sings while "Betty Martin" tiptoes around the room. (Use the child's own name, Betty Martin, or Billy Burton.)
- Add the extra chorus.
- Change the name to call another child to tiptoe.
- After a few children have demonstrated, the class sings and tiptoes to the whole song (in their own spaces.)

Enrichment:

Change the tiptoe to "walk, walk" and "walk-a-walk"; for a march, change to "left, right" and "left-a-right-a"; for running change to "run, run" and "run-a-run-a." For galloping, skipping, sliding, or skating, change the song to Hey o Bet - ty Mar - tin.

Related Activities:

One child may play this two tone bell accompaniment for the first part. (C F)

Hey Betty Martin

Traditional

ONE DAY ONE FOOT KEPT MOVING

Grades: K – 2

Focus: Coordinating melody, movement, words.

Materials: Arm's length space for each child.

Procedure:

This is a cumulative song with locomotor movements. It will be easier for some children than for others, depending on where they are in their coordination-growth pattern.

- Children stand.
- Sing the first verse together, everyone moving one foot in some way.
- Add the "one hand, one head" verses with movement.
- Continue with "two hands" verse.
- Continue with "two feet" verse. This will start the children dancing to the song.
- Repeat the "two feet" verse, singing with spirit.
- End the dancing with a quiet verse "And then they all stopped moving".

The children will want to do it again.

Use these verses for nonlocomotor movements: "Today we all are bending (stretching, twisting, rocking, swaying, lifting)." Choose verses from these, alternating rather than accumulating verses. End the song with "And now we all are falling, and all are lying still."

Enrichment:

- For a holiday dance, children may wear jingle bells on their ankles and wrists. As the movement increases so does the jingling.

- For a ribbon dance, children may wear streamers around their wrists (and perhaps, a head band).

One day one foot kept mov - ing, kept mov - ing, kept mov - ing,

One day one foot, one hand, one head kept mov - ing, Heigh-O, Heigh-O, Heigh - O.

BLUEBIRD

Grades: K – 2

Focus: Introducing a circle game; Verses in music.

Materials: Ample space for circle.

Procedure:

This game was popular with children throughout the nineteenth and early twentieth centuries. Children still enjoy it. Early settlers probably brought it with them from the British Isles. It may be played sitting or standing.

In contrast to many lively singing games, this is a slow, relaxed activity. It gives the children ample time to learn the routine of the game and prepares them for more vigorous and complicated games.

Directions

- Form a circle with space between the children.

Verse One

- One child is the "Bluebird" and weaves in and out of the circle between the children.
- On "Oh, Johnny, I am tired," the "Bluebird" stops in back of one child.

Verse Two

- The "Bluebird" pats the shoulder of the chosen child.
- On the last phrase, the "Bluebird" takes the place of the chosen one who then becomes the next "Bluebird."

Bluebird

Verse Two
Take a little one and pat him (her) on the shoulder, (three times)
Oh, Johnny, I am tired.

Movement and Mood

ALL THE PRETTY LITTLE HORSES

Grades: K – 3

Focus: Gentle movements and mood in music.

Materials: (Optional) Bells D̲ E F G A B♭ C (D̄).

Procedure:

This quiet song in the Aeolian mode is dominated by an almost complete downward natural minor scale, starting on high C. This passage occurs four times. This downward scale played on bells (or sung) makes a good introduction.

The promise of a coach and horses reflects the fantasy of bygone days.

- Sing the entire song.
- Sing the downward scale phrase with the children.
- Encourage singing on repeats.
- Sing the entire song to the children; have them sing the downward passages as a chorus.
- End the session with gently swaying or rocking movements as an accompaniment. The action may be extended by dramatizing a lullaby.

All the Pretty Little Horses

Southern Lullaby

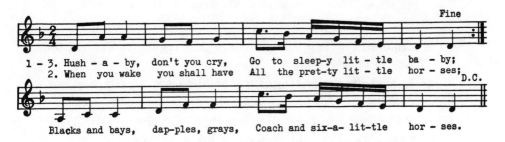

Enrichment:

1. Expand the bell playing. Play the choral phrase as an accompaniment and also when it occurs in the song.
2. Act out a dream sequence fulfilling the promise of the lullaby.

Related Activities:

Sing other American lullabies such as "Hush Little Baby" and
"Counting Stars."

CHICKEN REEL

Grades: K – 2; 3 – 8

Focus: Grades K – 2: Large muscle—whole body movements; Grades
3 – 8: Contrasting melodies—planning the movement.

Materials: Melody instrument; whistle or sing.

Procedure:

This is a favorite fiddle tune with a very tricky melody and
rhythm. Supposedly, these words fit the first part of the tune, "Oh,
nev-er troub-le troub-le 'til the troub-le troub-les you." It is also a
good whistling or "tum-tu-tum" tune.

The first two measures are repeated in part to make phrase one.
The fifth and sixth measures are repeated to make phrase two. You
may repeat either or both phrases as many times as you like to match
your dance. The piece ends on either phrase.

Grades K – 2

- Children practice their whistling as they dance in their own
way to phrase one.
- Repeat phrase one until the children set a pattern in their
dancing.
- Children dance (and whistle if they like) phrase two. Repeat
phrase two until the movement takes on a pattern.
- Put the two phrases together as one dance.
- A simpler dance is to repeat the first dance but reverse the
action to show a change in the music.

- A more formal dance may be had by moving to these directional words.
  Phrase 1: "Oh, dance around and dance around and dance around the room."
  (repeat)
  Phrase 2: "Put out your foot and dance around the room."
  (repeat)
  "Turn up your toe", "hands on your hips"; "go to your left"; etc.)

Grades 3 - 8

- A student instrumentalist may play the piece; students may whistle or sing; or the teacher may play it on any available instrument. Clapping and foot-tapping give spirit to the dance. Use any two basic square dance patterns, one for each phrase or repeat.
- The piece may be brought up-to-date by adding a constant drum beat (♩ ♩ ♩ ♩). Use current dance steps.

Related Activities:

Listen to other fiddle tunes; Folkways records, 2376 *Walkie in the Parlor;* 2434 *The 37th Old-time Fiddler's Convention;* 2390 *Friends of Old Time Music.*

Chicken Reel

Indian Music

THE MOCCASIN SONG

The Ojibway or Chippewa Indians are natives of Michigan, Wisconsin and Minnesota. This children's song (and dance) is an expression of pleasure in wearing moccasins, perhaps new ones.

It is quite usual for all children to sing and dance about ordinary objects and everyday events that give them pleasure.

The compound meter signature, 3/4 2/4, means that one measure of 3/4 is followed by one measure of 2/4, making a short phrase of five beats. Be sure to accent the first beat of each phrase.

THE MOCCASIN SONG

Lesson One: The Song

Grades: K – 6

Focus: Learning the song and feeling the rhythm.

Materials: (Optional) a small drum.

Procedure:

If you use a small hand drum, play it softly so it will not detract from the song.

- Present the first phrase well accented.
- Repeat it several times with the children singing along.
- Without interruption go on to phrase two.
- Sing the first two phrases all together.
- Move to phrases three and four, using the same routine, combining them after a few repeats.
- Repeat the entire song with the children singing along.

It may take more than one session for this song to become fixed in the children's memory.

Enrichment:

Use a song flute or recorder to accompany the singers. The accompaniment may consist of the entire melody, or only one phrase repeated throughout.

Related Activity:

Listen to Indian music; *Songs and Dances of Great Lake Indians*, Folkways 4003.

The Moccasin Song

**Ojibway Indians
(Chippewa)**

Moc-ca-sins I am a-wear-ing, Moc-ca-sins I am a-wear-ing,

Moc-ca-sins I am a-wear-ing, Moc-ca-sins I am a-wear-ing.

Indian Words

Mu-je mu-ke-sin au yaw yon.

THE MOCCASIN SONG

Lesson Two: The Dance

Grades: K – 2; 3 – 6

Focus: Creating a dance for the song.

Materials: Small drums; one or more shakers.

Procedure:

The melody is different for each phrase but the rhythm is exactly the same.

Grades K – 2

- Review the song, emphasizing the accent and encouraging a whole body movement such as swaying (slow) or stretching.
- Direct attention to what the feet can do to show off the moccasins.
- Each child dances his dance. Very little room will be required. (Later, it may develop into leaping etc. which requires extended space.)
- End the session with solo and group dances on repeats.

Grades 3 – 6

A simple line or follow-the-leader dance may consist of one pattern repeated for each phrase. This may be varied by inserting solo patterns for some phrases.

- Suggestions for steps
  1. Take large careful steps throughout the song, carrying a shaker in each hand and swinging arms to the rhythm.
  2. Step, step, step, pat, pat.
  3. Alternate suggestions 1 and 2.
- Start the dancing with version 1. Emphasize accents at the beginning of each phrase with a drum beat.
- Repeat the song using version 2.
- Discuss the original steps and encourage the children to demonstrate their steps.
- Plan a routine of steps growing out of the discussion and demonstrations.
- All dancers carry shakers and/or drums.

NAVAJO HAPPY SONG

Grades: 2 – 3

Focus: Dancing musical phrases.

Materials: Floor space.

Procedure:

The title of the song gives the clue for the dance. The words of the first phrase "Hi yo hi yo ip si ni yah" are repeated in all four phrases but the melody is different in the first three. The last phrase is a repetition of phrase three. The last two measures form a coda, or extra, and final, ending.

Keep the identity of the phrases when working out the dance. Even a slight pause between phrases can accomplish this.

Free Dance

- Sing the entire song to get the feeling of the rhythm.
- Sing the first phrase.
- Repeat it and move to the beat.
- Move to each phrase, then put the phrases together.
- After this experimental dance, discuss the results.
- At another session the steps may be quite different.

Patterned Dance

Follow the leader. In this dance, the variation is in the hand and body motions. The slow tiptoe step remains the same until the coda.

Phrase 1: Stand erect, arms bent, elbows alternately keeping the beat.

Phrase 2: Hold arms high, hands keeping the beat, and eyes following the hand motions.

Phrase 3: Bend body forward, elbows keeping the beat.

Phrase 4: Repeat phrase 3.

Coda: Stamp, and indicate the accent with the elbows. Leap up on "Yah!"

Enrichment:

Children work out another patterned dance that may be combined with the one above.

Creativity and Imagination

THE SYNCOPATED CLOCK
by
Leroy Anderson

Grades: 1 – 4

Focus: Dramatic movement.

Materials: Recording, *Music of Leroy Anderson* – Mercury; Wood block.

Procedure:

- Listen to the music about the funny clock.
- Discuss the clock sounds. Verbalize ideas. Encourage descriptions of the sounds, the clock.
- Demonstrate the wood block.
- Experiment with motions that parallel the sounds.
- Put movement and music together. (The wood block may be used as an accompaniment.) Dramatize the kinds of clocks they hear.

Enrichment:

A formal clock dance is a natural outcome of this lesson.

ON THE FOURTH OF JULY

Dance This Poem into a Picture

Grades: 2 – 5

Focus: Coordinating movement, rhythm, words.

Materials: Floor space.

Procedure:

On the Fourth of July we fly the flag.
Blow. How the breezes blow.

The bands parade along the main street.
Drums and all the horns play.

A man makes a speech about 1776.
He mentions George Washington, first.

The chicken is fried and the ice cream is cold.
It's picnic time. Let's eat.

The action verbs hold the key to the movements and the children proceed toward a picture.

- Read the entire poem.
- Discuss it, verse by verse, encouraging the children to tell of their Fourth of July experiences.
- Children get ready for action (stand apart at arm's length).
- Read the poem again and encourage free rhythmic description. At the end of each verse the children hold the action (freeze) as it is on the last word.

To present this in a program, divide the children into four groups, one group for each verse. One child may be the reader or one child from each group may read the verse as the group interprets it. At the end of the poem there will be a tableau. To make it more elaborate, children may carry flags, wear head bands, or spread a picnic cloth on the floor.

Enrichment:

Listen to *The Fourth of July* by Charles Ives.

GOODBYE OLD PAINT

Grades: 2 – 3

Focus: Slow sauntering step; dramatization.

Materials: Wood block or coconut cymbals.

Procedure:

This cowboy song has the typical slow easy rhythm characteristic of cowboy songs. The slow sauntering movement of the cowboy and Old Paint and Old Fan makes a little parade.

- Use the wood block or coconut cymbals to set the step—a-clomp, a-clomp, a-clomp.

- The cowboy on Old Paint leads Old Fan as the class (or little Annie) waves goodbye and sings.
- Informally divide the class into partners.
- Everyone sings as they "leave Cheyenne" and head toward "Montan."
- Those who do not want to be cowboys may be the accompaniment saying "a-clomp" or playing the instruments.

Enrichment:

Sing other cowboy songs like "The Night Herding Song."

Goodbye Old Paint

Cowboy Song

Refrain   Bb   Gm   F7   Bb Fine

Good — bye, Old   Paint,   I'm a - leav-in' Chey - enne.

Verses   Bb   Gm   Bb   F7   Bb   D.C.

My   foot in the   stir-rup, my   po - ny won't stand,
I'm a leav-in' Chey - enne,   I'm   off for Mon - tan.

Verse 2: I'm a-rid-in' Old Paint, I'm leadin' Old Fan.
          Good-bye lit-tle An-nie, I'm off for Chey-enne.

Play Party Dances

LOVE SOMEBODY

This simple tune has two parts of eight measures each. In addition to being a good song, the strong rhythm makes it ideal for any easy partner dance. It is probably an old fiddle tune. Children usually sing the song as they dance. It is reminiscent of the English and French contradance (contredanse) that later developed into the quadrille. Basically, a contradance is done with two lines of dancers moving in opposite directions.

LOVE SOMEBODY

Lesson One: Two-Part Form

Grades: K – 2

Focus: Recognition of two-part form; matching the dance to the two parts.

Materials: Floor space.

Procedure:

- Learn the song, if not familiar.
- Sing the first part and experiment with movement. One pattern may be repeated for the four phrases.
- Sing and move to the first part.
- Sing the second part.
- Experiment with movement for this part. Discuss the differences between the parts. The movement may be as simple as changing the direction of the first pattern.
- Sing and dance the whole song.

LOVE SOMEBODY

Lesson Two: Line Dance

Grades: 3 – 6

Focus: Partner dancing in the country dance idiom.

Material: (Optional) Chording instrument for accompaniment.

Procedure:

- Children take partners.
- They stand in two rows, four steps apart, with partners facing.

Part One

Measures 1 – 2: Four steps forward
Measures 3 – 4: Four steps backward
Measures 5 – 6: Four steps forward
Measures 7 – 8: Four steps backward

Part Two

While others sing and clap, the number one partners, or the head couple, move in back of their lines and arrive at the other end in time to face each other and to stamp their feet on "loves me, too."
Repeat the dance until each couple has moved to the other end.

Love Somebody

Play Party Song

OLD BRASS WAGON

Lesson One: Making a Circle

Grades: K – 2

Focus: Making a circle, turning left or right.

Materials: Singers, caller, or instrumental accompaniment.

Procedure:

- Children join hands. Lead them into a circle. Sing "See us dance, the old brass wagon."
- "Circle to the left." Stand in the middle and snap left fingers or make a pointing gesture to direct the line.
- "Circle to the right." Gesture to help them move to the right.
- Repeat these two verses until they are learned.
- Lead the circle back to their seats while singing "Promenade home."

OLD BRASS WAGON

Lesson Two: Traditional Patterns

Grades: 3 – 8

Focus: Learning the basic figures.

Materials: Space for dancing.

Procedure:

Each verse features one of the basic patterns.

Verse 1: Circle to the left

Verse 2: Circle to the right

Verse 3: Swing, oh swing

Verse 4: Promenade around (left)

Verse 5: Swing your partners

Verse 6: Break and swing

Verse 7: Promenade home

Cir-cle to the left the   old brass wa-gon, Cir-cle to the left the old brass wa-gon

Cir-cle to the left, the   old brass wa - gon, You're the one my   dar - ling.

SOURWOOD MOUNTAIN

Grades: 4 – 8

Focus: Square Dance; Rhythm on Bones (Optional).

Materials: Floor space; (Optional) Bones or claves; Melody and/or chording instruments.

Procedure:

This song has several versions and melodic variations. This is probably the most common.

Directions for the square dance:

- Form a square made up of four couples.
- Designate one couple as first or head couple.
- The couple to their right is couple two, couple directly across is couple three, and couple to their left is couple four.

Verse 1

Phrases 1–2: First couple walks to second couple; all join hands and circle 4 steps to left, then 4 steps to right.

Phrases 3–4: Drop hands; hook elbows and swing opposite partners around once; return to partner and swing around once.

Verse 2

Repeat the dance with couple three.

Verse 3

Repeat the dance with couple four.

Verse 4

Couple one is back in its original place. On the call "allemande left," the boys face the girls to their left, grasp left hands and circle completely around until each is facing his own partner. Begin a grand right and left. Extend the right hand to your partner, pass him by and continue to the next person, extending your left hand. Continue until each person has returned to his original partner. Girls reverse direction and all promenade back to their original place in the square.

Playing Bones

Use the rhythm for "Chicken crowin' on sourwood mountain."

Sourwood Mountain

Southern Mountain Song

Chick-en crow-in' on Sour-wood Moun-tain, Hey de ing dang did-dle al-lay day
So man-y pret-ty girls I can't count 'em, Hey de ing dang did-dle al-lay day
My true love she lives in Letch-er, Hey de ing dang did-dle al-lay day
She won't come and I won't fetch her, Hey de ing dang did-dle al-lay day.

2. My true love's a blue-eyed daisy, etc.
   If I don't get her I'go crazy, etc.
   Big dogs bark and little ones bite you, etc.
   Big girls court and little ones slight you, etc.

3. My true love lives by the river, etc.
   A few more jumps and I'll be with her, etc.
   My true love lives up the hollow, etc.
   She won't come and I won't follow, etc.

4. Same as verse 1.

Rounds for Dancing

Singing rounds is at once a pleasure and a challenge. Good round singing results from a foundation of knowing the song well in unison. A slight emphasis on the rhythm helps when the song is sung as a round.

Moving to a round is similar to singing a round. The movements are planned and executed in unison first. Each part of the round has a separate movement sequence.

In performance, the movement may accompany the singing or may be done independently as a separate verse. A full-length dance is also possible.

ROUNDS FOR DANCING

Grades: 4 – 8

Focus: Planning and executing the movement for rounds; (contrapuntal movement).

Materials: Large floor space.

Procedure:

Steps in planning the movement:
Preliminary:
1. Learn to sing the round in unison.
2. After first determining the number of times the round is to be repeated, sing the round in parts.

Activity:
1.(A) Sing part one, emphasizing the rhythmic pattern with clapping.

(B) Join hands and, moving forward, step to the rhythm of the words. Be sure that everyone starts on the same foot.

(C) Repeat steps A and B for each part of the round.

2. Teacher directed, or move to 3.

(A) Demonstrate a movement sequence for each part.

(B) Children copy these movements. Rehearse this as an unison dance.

(C) Movement sequences and singing are done as a round.

3. Child created.
   With the background of a well-learned round and practice in stepping to the words, most children will be ready to create movement sequences. This may be done by individuals or by small groups made up of one or two children on each part.

ROW, ROW, ROW YOUR BOAT

1. Very easy
   Measures 1 – 2: Slow walk
   Measures 3 – 4: Fast walk
   When programmed as a round, the slow and fast parts will happen at the same time.
2. With Action of Hands and Feet
   Measures 1 – 2: Slow walk; hands doing rowing action, first right, then left.
   Measures 3 – 4: Fast walk and rowing action to match.

WHERE IS JOHN?

Measures 1 – 2: Walk with arms out, turning to each side.

Measures 3 – 4: Walk, pantomine "Cut, cut, cuduckit."

Measures 5 – 6: Walk with arms out, turning to each side.

Measures 7 – 8: Walk, pantomime "Moo, moo, moo."

Measures 9 – 12: Walk in a small circle; cup hands and pantomime calling "John."

Shout the word "Where" each time it occurs.

This may be accompanied by the chord sequence repeated over and over as three or more people sing the round.

Row, Row, Row Your Boat
(Two- or Four-Part Round)

Where Is John?
(Three-Part Round)

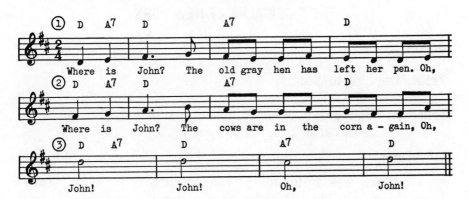

Where is John? The old gray hen has left her pen. Oh,

Where is John? The cows are in the corn a-gain, Oh,

John!   John!   Oh,   John!

Patterned Movement

THE SIDEWALKS OF NEW YORK

Grades: 5 – 8

Focus: Learning to waltz.

Materials: Keyboard or other chromatic instrument; If a guitar is used, dancers may sing the song.

Procedure:

This song was written in 1894 by a vaudeville performer and a businessman who liked to write verses. Later, this popular song became the unofficial song for New York City. Two New York politicians, Mayor James J. Walker and Alfred E. Smith (who was nominated for the presidency at the Democratic national convention in 1924), used this song.

The street scene described in the song was typical of New York in the late nineteenth century when neighbors gathered in the streets to escape the summer heat.

The triple meter makes this a good piece for learning to waltz.

- Review the song.
- Point out the triple meter and the accent on count one. Sing and tap foot on count one; swing arms for each measure. This helps the students feel the rhythm.
- Teach the steps by demonstrating with your back to the class; the students follow the steps without music. Count 1 2 3 slowly.
- Repeat several times, giving students ample time to learn the steps.
- Students dance (alone) to the music played on the keyboard or as they sing the song.
- Later, teach the steps moving backward instead of forward.
- After this is learned, practice the dance as a partner dance.

How to Waltz

Count 1 – Right foot takes a relatively long step forward.

Count 2 – Left foot takes a short sidestep inward.

Count 3 – Bring the right foot beside the left foot.

The next pattern will begin on the left foot.
The dance continues, patterns alternating between left and right foot.

The Sidewalks of New York

Charles B. Lawlor   James W. Blake

East side,   west   side,   all   a - round   the   town,_____

The   tots sang   "Ring   a   Ros - ie," "Lon-don   Bridge is   fall-ing   down."_____

Boys and girls to - geth - er,_____   Me   and   Ma-mie O' - Rorke,

Tripped the   light   fan - tas - tic   on   the   side-walks of New   York. _____

STARS AND STRIPES FOREVER
by
John Philip Sousa

Lesson One

Grades: K – 3

Focus: Informal marching; Recognition of changes in the music.

Materials: Recording or instrumental accompaniment; (Optional) Paper flags made by the children.

Procedure:

- Present the piece, suggesting that children listen for changes.
- Choose a leader.
- March to the music.

- The leader may indicate changes in the music by (1) holding up a flag, (2) changing direction, or by (3) changing the kind of stepping (high stepping, stepping in place).
- At the Trio, the leader begins to move the line back to the starting place.

Lesson Two

Grades: 4 – 8

Focus: Staging a class marching pattern culminating with choral singing.

Materials: Recording or instrumental accompaniment.

Procedure:

The form of this piece is:

> Introduction (4 measures)
> A (16 measures)
> A (16 measures)
> B (16 measures)
> B (16 measures)
> Trio (32 measures)

The marching pattern given here is basic in design, yet effective as a class program number in a large place such as a gymnasium or playground. Outline each pattern carefully so that it is well-learned before formations are attempted.

> Introduction: Stand in formation, at the back of the stage right in 4 lines, 4 abreast (total 16).

A – March across the back of the stage. At the last measure, make a quarter-turn to the right.

A – March forward downstage. At the last measure, make a quarter-turn to the right.

B – March across the front of the stage. At the last measure, make a quarter-turn to the *left* (to face the audience).

B – Take small side steps to the left (to center the group). Trio – Sing, standing in formation.
To exit after the performance, make a quarter-turn to the right to the corner, a quarter-turn right again, and exit at the back (original entrance).

Alternate plan (no singing)

A – same

A – same

B – March across the front of the stage. At the last measure, make a quarter-turn to the right.

B – March toward the back of the stage, make a large circle and move back to the original entrance place.

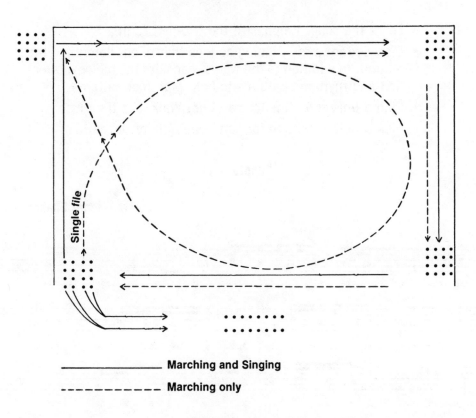

——————————— **Marching and Singing**

– – – – – – – – – **Marching only**

SIMPLE GIFTS

Grades: 4 – 8

Focus: Planning and performing a marching or dancing formation or a drill team routine to go with the melody, rhythm, and words of the song.

Materials: Optional—instrumental accompaniment.

Procedure:

This song of the Shaker religious sect is, perhaps, the best known of their hymns. Not only is it a song, but is also a dance. Intricate routines and patterns are sometimes created. Aaron Copland considered this song a bit of Americana and included it in the ballet *Appalachian Spring.*

These teaching suggestions may be used for several short sessions.

- Learn the song. Emphasize the two-part form.
- Discuss the words, finding actions that might determine the routine. In addition to the words, consider the melody, direction and rhythmic patterns to help plan foot patterns.
- Plan a unison routine for part one. Walk it to the music.
- Plan a unison routine for part two. Walk or dance it.

Simple Gifts

Traditional Shaker Song

- To vary the dance, one group may do part one, and a second group may do the other part or repeat.

Enrichment:

For a programmed activity, two groups may plan different patterns. These may be combined in performance, giving the impression of a much more complicated routine.

Related Activities:

Listen to *Appalachian Spring.*

HAWAIIAN BOAT SONG

Lesson One

Grades: K – 2

Focus: Feeling the up and down lilt of the melody and the strong, gentle rhythm (imitative rhythms).

Materials: (Optional) Ukulele or autoharp accompaniment; Picture of an outrigger canoe.

Procedure:

The state of Hawaii is a group of islands in the Pacific Ocean. In the bays you can often see outrigger canoes riding the rolling waves.

- Sing the song, swaying back and forth.
- Feel how the canoe moves forward as it glides over the gentle waves.
- Designate floor space for the "water."
- Accompany the singing with chords as the children move in their own way. Emphasize a light lift on the strong pulses.
- Repeat the song as the "boats" glide back to their seats.

Enrichment:

An older child or the teacher may demonstrate how the ukulele is played. Show pictures of Hawaiian scenes.

Related Activities:

Play recordings of early Hawaiian chants and songs with authentic instruments.

HAWAIIAN BOAT SONG

Lesson Two

Grades: 3 – 6

Focus: Composing a hand hula (coordinating hand motions and words).

Materials: (Optional) Ukulele or autoharp for accompaniment.

Procedure:

The hula is a traditional dance of the old Hawaiian culture. The hand motions tell the story of the song. Children's hand hulas are often danced while sitting. (The children kneel and sit on their heels.) When the hand hula is done standing, a foot rhythm is added, quite often a side step done in place.

- Learn the song.
- Discuss each noun and action verb. Create actions suggested by the words or use the suggestions below.

    boat – open palms together
    gliding – arm moving in slight up and down wavy motions
    sea – hands stretch wide
    ukuleles – imitation of the strumming

Hawaiian Boat Song

Folk Song

Enrichment:

- Teach ukulele chords G and D7.
- Make the ukulele available for individual practice.
- Add more verses: We're floating on Hawaiian waters,
                                    We're floating on the blue, blue sea.

Related Activities:

Listen to traditional Hawaiian music.

PART FIVE

Creating American Music

BALLADS

Ballad of the Country Frog
Ballad of the Bicycle

CREATING YOUR OWN BALLAD OPERA

Betsy: or Comicat and the Sampler
Tom Goes West

RHYTHM

Johnny Get Your Hair Cut
Rhythm Groupings in 9/8 Meter
Creating a Hula

FORM IN MUSIC

Creating a Folk Song Rondo
Creating a Percussion Rondo
Creating Your Own Blues

SCALES: BASIS FOR COMPOSING

Summer Night in Alaska
Riddle Song
Nevada Sunrise

ROUNDS, VOCAL CHORDING, DESCANTS, EMBELLISHMENTS

The Band in the Park
Shalom Chaverim
Down in the Valley
Oh When the Saints Go Marching In

TRADITIONAL CHORDS

Fanfare for an American Hero/Heroine
Creating Your Own Drum and Bugle Corps
Traditional Folk Song Cadence

NEW SOUNDS

A Storm in the Rockies

New Sounds on the Autoharp

Creating New Sounds with
Tape Recorders

Twelve Tones

THE AMERICAN HERITAGE

Creating an American Medley

George Washington and the
Cherry Tree

A Fourth of July Parade

America the Beautiful
(Word Pictures)

The Gettysburg Address
(Background Music)

Creating American Music

The basic elements of sound—duration, pitch and texture—are the raw materials of which music is made. *Duration* is developed and organized into endless combinations of rhythmic patterns in a variety of tempi. *Pitch* becomes melody moving up or down in large or small skips or steps or microsteps, sometimes lingering on one tone. The *texture* of sound is evident in the natural sounds of the universe, the human voice, instrumentation, and in artifically produced sounds, as on a synthesizer. The whole spectrum of sound that can be heard by the human ear or felt in pulse vibrations is the playground of the composer and performer.

* * * * * * * * * * * * * * *

These lessons dealing with creating new American music emphasize the basic elements of music. Traditional American music such as ballads, strophic songs, ballad opera, work songs, music for dancing, blues, improvisation, program or descriptive pieces, modally oriented music, and electronically produced sounds are used as vehicles of creativity. Sometimes creative movement, dramatic play, story telling, choric reading, and exploration of instruments commonly used in America are also present.

Some late twentieth century music is more universal than national. The new styles in music and the techniques of composing are not always unique to America but are a part of a developing worldwide awareness of sound possibilities. However, new American compositions readily reflect the variety and richness of American life. Young Americans, using basic techniques and materials to create their first music, will acquire an understanding of how to develop their own musical ideas and talents.

Ballads

In the times when there were few books and most people did not read, story telling and ballads (telling stories with song) were very common. Not only were tales and ballads a means of communication, with wandering entertainers telling of events in faraway places, they were also a major source of entertainment. Old folk ballads were about brave deeds, unrequited love, occasionally about a happy love affair, and, of course, about humorous happenings. Many were spontaneous singing-dancing songs with singers telling the story and dancers acting it out in verses. The audience joined in on the refrains, sometimes singing, sometimes singing and dancing.

Accompaniments have varied through the years. The viola da gamba, lute, recorder, finger drums and cymbals, the concertina, zither, tambourine, harmonica, fiddle, banjo, reed organ, bones, improvised instruments, and, especially, the guitar, have all been used at one time or another. Simple hand-clapping and foot-stamping are also good for keeping the rhythm.

Early American ballads were patterned after the European ballads. In New England, ballads were patterned after the English and Scottish; in the South, many ballads were like the French or Spanish.

THE BALLAD OF THE COUNTRY FROG
(Oh! Susanna)

Grades: 3– 6

Focus: Creating a humorous ballad, using a familiar tune, (Oh! Susanna); Rhythm and rhyme in poetry.

Materials: Chalkboard or erasable chart paper.

Procedure:

The verses of "Oh! Susanna" move in traditional ballad meter with alternating accented and unaccented beats.

To get the ballad started, use these two verses:

> **One**
> Oh, in the field where flowers grow
> And a little stream flows by,
> Was a green and spotted country frog
> Who croaked, "Galump, galih."

Chorus:
One little froggie, who croaked, "Galump, galih,"
Just a green and spotted country frog
Who croaked, "Galump, galih."

Two
Now, the green and spotted country frog
Left the flowers and the stream,
And he hopped afar to the city streets
And croaked "Galump, galih."

Complete the ballad with verses that tell what happened to the frog. Possibilities: He crossed the street in traffic; A dog snapped at his head; A boy punched him with a stick.

THE BALLAD OF THE BICYCLE

Grades: 2 – 6

Focus: Writing words for a ballad tune in 6/8 meter; Ballad with conversational verse and chorus.

Materials: Chalkboard or erasable chart paper.

Procedure:

- Sing the first verse and chorus. (Stress counts 1 and 4.)
- Memorize the chorus.
- Write other verses that tell what happened to the bicycle.

The Ballad of the Bicycle

Old tune

Oh lend me your bicycle, lend me your bike,
Bicycle, bicycle, lend me your bike.
I'll clean it and oil it and polish your bike,
I'll take care and bring back your bike.

Chorus:
And when will I see you, (Tom), riding my bike?
Bicycle, bicycle, riding my bike?
And when will I see you, (Tom), riding my bike.
Oh, when will I see you again?

Creating Your Own Ballad Opera

Write the plot of your opera, incorporating as many songs as you like. Keep the action and the music moving at a fast pace. Change the words of songs, use them for background, dance to them, create comic routines to them. Do anything with the music that helps the story. End your ballad opera with a chorus and dance. Review the lesson on ballad opera and *Flora: or Hob in the Well.*

BETSY: OR COMICAT AND THE SAMPLER

A Multi-lesson Project

Grades: 4 – 6

Focus: Completing the story and dialogue; selecting the music and adding appropriate words; learning songs and dances; the Donkey game; staging.

Materials: A reasonable repertoire of songs. (Appropriate music may be found in this book.)

Procedure:

Partial Story Suggestions

Betsy, a little colonial girl, is working on a sampler, embroidering the alphabet and numbers across the top. As she sews, she hums "Yankee Doodle." Her mother comes in to inspect her sewing. Comicat is asleep at Betsy's feet.

Outside, the children sing and play a game of tag, ("Sweetly Sings the Donkey"). Jonathan and the other children call to Betsy "Leave the sewing on the shelf, come out and play with us etc." ("Sweetly Sings". . .) Betsy's mother says that Betsy must finish embroidering the letter "C" before she goes out to play. Then her mother leaves the room, chanting a riddle for Betsy to solve while she sews; "Patch on patch without any stitches, If you give me the answer I'll buy some britches." The answer is a cabbage patch. (From the book *Ring Around the Moon* by Edith Fowke, © 1977 by Edith Fowke. Published by Prentice-Hall, Inc. Used by permission.)

Comicat gets up and stretches. Betsy says, "Comicat, do your funny dance for me." The cat rolls over, stretches his paws, then leaps around the room. Betsy laughs, claps and sings. Comicat looks up at Betsy and blinks. Encouraged by Betsy's approval, he jumps up on her lap, tangling the embroidery thread with his paws. In a panic, Comicat jumps down again and runs out the door, dragging the sampler with him (background music by children playing).

Betsy runs after Comicat. The children leave the game to chase Comicat who climbs into a tree with the sampler still trailing after him. Betsy sings to Comicat to calm him, "Comicat, Comicat, please come down here; Comicat Comicat, please come down here; Comicat, Comicat, please come down here, Please come to Betsy." (Tune: "Bluebird.")

Finish the story. Solve the problem, get the sampler back, placate the mother, etc. Use at least one song while solving the problems. End with a chorus and dance. (This may be a repetition of the game song.)

Enrichment:

Sing "Sweetly Sings the Donkey" as a round.

Sweetly Sings the Donkey

Traditional

Leave the sewing on the shelf; come out and play with us.
Sewing is for winter time; come out and play with us.
Come and play; Come out and play with us.

The Game:

1. Children stand in a line facing a goal twenty to twenty-five feet away. One child is "it" (the donkey).
2. Children sing the song. On the last "Hee-haw" the donkey leaves the line and runs toward the opposite goal.
3. Children in the line run after the donkey. The one who catches the donkey before he reaches the goal, becomes the next donkey. If no one catches the donkey, he remains the donkey for the next game.

TOM GOES WEST
(A Plot to be Developed into a Ballad Opera)
A Multi-lesson Project

Grades: 4 – 7

Focus: Developing the plot into a ballad opera; scenes, dialogue, songs, dances, staging.

Materials: Reasonable repertoire of songs and square or line dances. (Appropriate music may be found in this book.)

Procedure:

Suggested Plot

Tom and his family are moving west in a covered wagon. The wagon train stops by a creek for a night's rest before they leave the plains for the mountains. (Music, square dancing, play party games, singing.)

Tom stays overnight with his cousin Seth in his uncle's wagon. In the morning, he runs down to the creek for an early morning swim. The wagon train moves ahead without him. Tom's family think he is with his cousin. Seth thinks Tom has gone back to his family. (Music as the train moves ahead)

When Tom comes back to the campsite, he sees the wagon train in the distance. As he runs to catch up, he sprains his ankle and cannot run. To keep up his courage, he whistles and sings songs.

The next evening, Tom's family discover his absence. (Music in the background – "Old Brass Wagon," etc.) Tom's family and relatives meet to decide what to do. Seth offers to ride his pony back to look for Tom. (Singing "Old Hundredth" or other quiet song).

In the morning, Seth rides back, loses, then finds the trail left by the wagon wheels (songs of the land, a lonesome song – "Erie Canal," "Red River Valley," "Down in the Valley," etc.)

Seth finds Tom. They care for the pony, eat the food that Seth has brought (sing together), wrap themselves in the blanket Seth has carried, and sleep by the campfire. They hear night cries of buffalo and prairie wolves, and the squeaking of sparrows in the poplar trees.

The next morning, they ride ahead. Finally, at dusk, they catch up with the wagon train. The fiddler is tuning up, the singing and dancing has begun. There is a triumphant ride into camp. End with a chorus and dance.

Rhythm

JOHNNY, GET YOUR HAIR CUT

A Dance for Boys

Grades: K – 2

Focus: Dancing the song, creating new steps and new verses, and dramatizing the song.

Materials: (Optional) Improvised props for dramatization.

Procedure:

- Sing the song until it is familiar.
- Boys dance the song with their *feet.*
- Boys dance the song with feet and *hands*; then with feet, hands, *head.*
- Give opportunities for solo dancing.
- Add original verses at any time during the lesson.
- Dramatize the action, dancing at the same time.

Enrichment:

As a dance for girls, use "Janie" instead of "Johnny." Encourage girls to make up verses about good grooming.

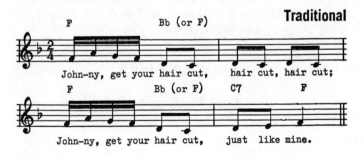

John-ny, get your hair cut, hair cut, hair cut;
John-ny, get your hair cut, just like mine.

RHYTHM GROUPINGS IN 9/8 METER

Variety in American Music

Grades: 5 – 8

Focus: Divisions of 9/8 meter; Comparison of these divisions; Creating new compound rhythms.

Materials: Chalkboard or chart paper; Small drum; "Down in the Valley;" "Blue Rondo a la Turk."

Procedure:

Rhythmic patterns and accents.

- Sing "Down in the Valley"
- Write the rhythm pattern.
- Sing the song again, tapping out the rhythm with fingers.
- One person taps out the rhythm on the drum.
- Listen to "Blue Rondo a la Turk"
- Write the rhythm pattern.
- Listen to the piece again. Tap out the rhythm with fingers and drum.
- Create other divisions of 9/8 meter and tap them on a drum. (Suggestions: 5 and 4; 4, 2, 3; 4, 4, and 1.)

Enrichment:

Using the newly created rhythmic divisions, play the rhythm on any of the black keys (piano or bells). Add tambourine or other available instruments in their own divisions of 9/8. The accents will come in different places and polyrhythms will result.

CREATING A HULA

Hawaiian Boat Song

Grades: 4 – 6

Focus: Creating verses and hulas to describe the verses.

Materials: Ipu (large hollow gourd). As a substitute for the ipu, slap a table top, the side of a drum or thighs.

Procedure:

The exotic flowers, beautiful beaches, tropical rain, green colorings of the mountains, volcanos, and other natural beauties of Hawaii will inspire other verses and actions.

- Review the melody of "Hawaiian Boat Song."
- Use the same melody and meter patterns for a new verse describing another beauty of the islands.
- Design hand motions to describe the new verse.
- One person may accompany the singing and dancing with the ipu or substitute sounds.

Form In Music

Music is organized into parts or sections. This gives opportunities for contrast, repetitions, musical description, variations.

Ternary form (A B A) is the most common form in music. The return of the A part reinforces the original statement of the music and provides a logical conclusion to the piece for the listener. One example of this is singing a chorus, a verse, and then returning to the chorus.

Rondo form is an extension of ternary form. Frequently, it is A B A C A, but it may vary in several ways. A section may vary slightly (A') when it returns; there may be several new parts, A B A C A D A E A, or fragments from sections may be combined for the ending.

CREATING A FOLK SONG RONDO

Grades: 4 – 6

Focus: Using familiar folk songs in a rondo.

Materials: (Optional) Rhythm sticks, small drum, jingle bells.

Procedure:

Review these three songs – "I'm Gonna' Sing," "Rock Island Line," "Jingle Bells."

- The A part – "I'm Gonna Sing"
  Sing the melody on "Ta – ta"
  Tap out the rhythm with fingertips on a hard surface, or with sticks.
- The B part – "Rock Island Line"
  Sing the words.
  Slap thighs for rhythm or use a drum.
- Repeat A
- The C part – "Jingle Bells" (chorus)
  Sing the words.
  Clap the rhythm or shake jingle bells.
- Repeat A part.

Enrichment:

- Tape the rondo for study.
- Use other songs to create another rondo.

CREATING A PERCUSSION RONDO

Grades: 4 – 6

Focus: Creating a rondo with contrasting rhythms.

Materials: At least four percussion instruments such as drums, sticks, tambourines, maracas, etc.

Procedure:

- Four students or four small groups create short rhythmic patterns. These may be original or they may be the rhythms of folk songs like the ones in the *Folk Song Rondo*.
- Each student or group performs its rhythm. (A B C D)
- Students perform the rhythms again, this time inserting the A part between each one.

CREATING YOUR OWN BLUES

Grades: 6 – 8

Focus: Exploring the blues formula; Improvisation within a chordal framework.

Materials: Any available instruments.

Procedure:

The blues is a kind of conversational music with a singer and several instruments talking about the same thing in their own way. Much of the "conversation" is made up as it goes along within the twelve-bar framework. Some of the characteristics of the blues are: the blues scale that flats the third and seventh of the major scale; tonic, subdominant and dominant harmonies with sevenths and ninths used generously; slow duple rhythm; and three-measure phrases.

- Instruments divide the four-part harmony and play the example exactly as written. (It may also be played on a keyboard or sung.)
- Keeping the same tempo and harmonies, singers and instruments repeat the example, varying the melodies (and rhythms) but always staying within the twelve-bar framework.
- Make each chord a seventh chord (C E(♭) G B (♭)), (F A C E (♭)) G B (♭) D F). Play and listen to the harmonies.
- Make each chord a ninth chord. Play and listen to the harmonies.
- Repeat the formula several times, varying it each time with solos, different forms of the chords, and individual suggestions, such as scale fragments, two melodies at once, repeated motives, using tones adjacent to the chord tones.

The Framework of the Traditional Blues

Scales: Basis For Composing

SUMMER NIGHT IN ALASKA
(In the Style of the Eskimo)

Grades: 4 – 6

Focus: Describing a scene with music, making up words and movement; the d minor scale.

Materials: Piano, bells, or other melody instrument.

Procedure:

Subjects for preliminary research and discussion: the long daylight of summer; the shadows; temperature; the Aurora Borealis.

- Play the d minor scale to set the mood.
- Play the first part of the song (to the dotted bar) on a melody instrument.
- Hum or sing that part with "la." Use a nasal quality.
- Sing or hum it again with the instrument.
- Put descriptive words to that part of the melody.
- The class or a small group may complete the melody. (If a melody does not develop, use the melody as given here.)
- Complete the words.

Summer Night in Alaska

Enrichment:

Write other verses.

THE RIDDLE SONG
Pentatonic Scale

Grades: 5 – 8

Focus: Exploring the pentatonic scale; Analyzing a pentatonic song; Creating an ostinato accompaniment (repeated pattern).

Materials: Staff on the chalkboard; Bells or Keyboard.

Procedure:

The pentatonic scale is made up of steps 1, 2, 3, 5, 6 (do, re, mi, sol, la) of the diatonic scale. The black keys on a piano make up one major pentatonic scale. Other patterns good for beginning composing are C D E G A, F G A C D, D E F♯ A B. Most pentatonic songs end on 1 or 6.

"The Riddle Song," a pentatonic song, uses only G A B D E of the G major scale. Characteristic pentatonic motives are "a cherry" (5 6 1) and the last "I gave my love" (3 2 1 6).

- Sing the song several times.
- Point out the characteristic motives.
- Write out the five tones of the song.
- Sing the song again with letters, numbers, syllables or a neutral syllable.
- Sing the entire song with the words.
- Play "A, G, E, D" on bells or keyboard as an introduction. Repeat it throughout the song as an accompaniment.
- Play any combination of the five notes contained in the song as an ostinato.

The Riddle Song

Kentucky Folk Song

(1) I gave my love a cher-ry that has no stone; I gave my love a chick-en that has no bone;

I gave my love a ring that has no end; I gave my love a ba-by, there's no cry-en.

(2) How can there be a cherry that has no stone?
How can there be a chicken that has no bone?
How can there be a ring that has no end?
How can there be a baby, there's no cryen?

(3) A cherry when it's bloomin' it has no stone;
A chicken when it's pippin' it has no bone;
A ring when it's rollin' it has no end;
A baby when it's sleepin' there's no cryen.

NEVADA SUNRISE
(Study in Whole-Tones)

Grades: 4 – 7

Focus: Whole-tone scale patterns as basis for composing; Nature as an inspiration for composing.

Materials: Keyboard or mallet bells; Music paper and/or tape recorder.

Procedure:

The whole-tone scale contains no drive toward a home tone or tone of finality. This lack of resolution toward a traditional final ending may leave the listener waiting for the expected ending which never arrives.

- To compose a whole-tone piece describing a Nevada sunrise, have the students discuss sunrises they have seen, sunrises on the desert, the colors, the horizon just before sunrise, the gradual dissolution of the colors.
- To establish a feeling for the whole-tone scale, students play each pattern several times.
- The class or small groups work on putting variations of the scale into phrases of a short descriptive composition.
- Write down or record the final version.

Two whole-tone patterns contain the twelve half-steps from C to C.

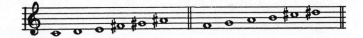

Rounds, Vocal Chording, Descants, Embellishments

THE BAND IN THE PARK
(A Two-Part Round)

Grades: 4 – 6

Focus: Creating a two-part round; F major scale, tonic and dominant chords.

Materials: Staff on chalkboard or erasable chart.

Procedure:

A round is composed so that when the tones sung on strong beats (in this case, one and three) are sung together, they harmonize. Generally, primary chords are the basis for this harmonization. However, melodies may include some non-chord tones.

In this unfinished round, measures 1, 2, 4, 5, 6, and 8 are based on the F or I chord. Measures 3 and 7 are built around the C or V or V_7 chord.

When filling in the rest of the melody, remember that the duration of each measure must equal four quarter notes (4/4).

- Copy the skeletal melody onto the chalkboard with part two directly below part one.
- Review the meaning of 4/4, writing examples if necessary.
- Students fill in the missing melody.
- Sing the melody with "bom, bom."
- Divide the class into two groups and slowly sing parts one and two together, listening carefully to the harmony.
- Discuss the melody and the harmony. Then make any changes suggested.
- Sing the melody with "too, too."
- Sing the melody until it is familiar.
- Divide the class into two groups. Group 1 sings "bom, bom." Group 2 sings "too, too."
- Sing it as a round.

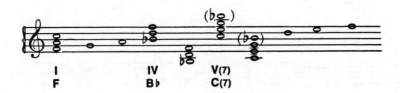

I	IV	V(7)
F	B♭	C(7)

SHALOM CHAVERIM
(Two- or Three-Part Round)

Grades: 6 – 8

Focus: Exploring the minor scale; Creating a vocal accompaniment (chording); Ethnic music becomes American.

Materials: Chalkboard or chart paper.

Procedure:

This round, brought to America by Jewish people from Europe, is now sung by Americans of many faiths. "Shalom" means peace; "Chaverim" means friends; "Lehitraot" means till we meet again.

This song uses all but one tone (B♭) of the d minor scale (natural). It can be harmonized with the d minor chord which dominates the song.

- Sing the song until it is familiar.
- Sing the d minor scale (natural).
- Sing the d minor chord, D – F – A.
- Humming or singing the neutral syllable "loo," one person sings D, one sings F, and another sings A. They sustain the chord.

- As the class sings the song, the chord is sung on the first count of each measure as an accompaniment.

Enrichment:

As an introduction, the three-part vocal accompaniment may be D-F-A; C-G-A; D-F-A.

DESCANT FOR DOWN IN THE VALLEY

Grades: 5 – 7

Focus: Creating a descant using the harmonic structure of a song.

Materials: A chording instrument; Bells or keyboard.

Procedure:

Originally, the word "descant" meant the treble or upper voice in part music. Now, it generally means an extra part above the melody, emphasizing the harmonic content of the song and sung or played on repetitions of the song. A vocal descant may use a neutral syllable such as "ah," words and phrases from the song, or words that complement the song.

- Review one verse of the song.
- One student plays the chord sequence while others hum the melody.
- As a beginning, sing the first "valley," "over," "blow dear," a third higher than the melody. (Do not sing other words.)

- Play the descant on the bells or keyboard on a second repeat.
- From this beginning, develop a more florid descant derived from the tonic-dominant harmonies.

Down in the Valley

Traditional

Down in the val - ley, the val - ley so low,

Hang your head ov - er, hear the wind blow,

Hear the winds blow dear, hear the winds blow,

Hang your head ov - er, hear the wind blow.

OH WHEN THE SAINTS GO MARCHING IN
(Embellishments)

Grades: 3 – 6

Focus: Improvising embellishments—short phrases, percussive, rhythmic sounds—to the song.

Materials: Small drum, guitar or autoharp.

Procedure:

This is a song from the Black culture of America. It is a hymn, a march, a dance. It is a good song for creating extra parts, responses, counter rhythms.

- Sing the song in strict rhythm. Keep a steady beat by slapping the knees, tapping a drum, or strumming the autoharp or guitar.

- Repeat the song several times, each time keeping the beat with a different body motion (head, shoulders, hands, feet).
- Use one or more of these motions to accompany the song and to fill in the rhythm on the long notes.
- On the long notes, some students may sing an extra phrase like "Oh, when the saints," picking up the melody on the next phrase.
- Pick out the most appropriate ones or take turns putting it all together.
- Perform the song with all the embellishments.

Enrichments:

- Harmonize the song by ear.
- Make up a counter melody.

Oh When the Saints Go Marching In

Traditional Spiritual

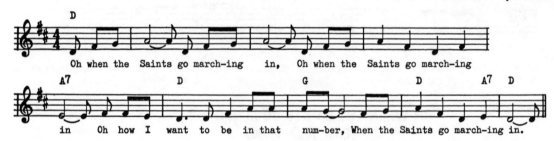

Traditional Chords

FANFARE FOR AN AMERICAN HERO/HEROINE

Grades: 1 – 3; 4 – 8

Focus: Grades 1 – 8: Honoring an outstanding American; Grades 4 – 8: Elements of a Fanfare and its uses.

Materials: Background material on the hero/heroine; Grades 1 – 3: Resonator or attached bells; Grades 4– 8: Any wind instruments, especially trumpets, played by members of the class; (Optional) Drum.

Procedure:

A fanfare is a short melody generally played by trumpets. It is usually based on a triad such as C-E-G. It is designed to draw the attention of a crowd, to introduce a ceremony or a great occasion, and, sometimes, to begin a march or other spirited piece of music.

A hero/heroine should be chosen—a distinguished person of great moral or physical courage.

Grades 1 – 3

- Children choose an American hero/heroine.
- Set all the C-E-G bells on a table. (On attached bells, identify the bells to be used with tape.)
- Several children take turns playing the bells as a tribute to the one to be honored.
- Leave bells available for individual exploration.
- At another session, children play their own fanfares.

Grades 4 – 8

- Choose the person to be honored.
- Discuss the meaning of hero/heroine and the reasons for choosing the person.
- Instrumentalists work in a small group to create a fanfare of about 4 measures. (Choose a chord, the meter. Experiment

with the chord tones and develop them into a melody.) A drum beat may be added.

Enrichment:

Listen to *Fanfare for the Common Man* (1942) by Aaron Copland

CREATING YOUR OWN DRUM AND BUGLE CORPS

Grades: 1 – 3

Focus: Individuals becoming a group; Making music with the mouth, sounds and drumming; Marching to their own music.

Materials: Big drum, several small drums, bell bars C̲ F̲ A C̅ F̅.

Procedure:

1. Children sing a bugle fanfare on "ta, ta" (the bells in order or their own tune based on the chord).
   Add a basic drum beat (1 – 2).
   Children march to self-made music, matching steps to the drum beats.

2. Ask for a volunteer to march (leader).
   Pick up the beat of the volunteer's marching on a drum.
   Give the large drum to a child who joins the original marcher.
   Give the small drums to other children who join the parade.
   Other children join the marching, singing the fanfare on "ta ta" as they march.

3. As an individual or small group project, children explore the bells of the F major chord with a directive to create a marching piece.
   Later, children carry bell bars and play their pieces as the other children follow, some playing drums.

TRADITIONAL FOLK SONG CADENCE
The Cadence March

Grades: K – 3; 4 – 8

Focus: K – 3: Establishing a marching beat; K – 8: Recognizing changing chords; 4 – 8: Analyzing the traditional cadence.

Materials: One or more autoharps.

Procedure:

The tones of the major scale may be numbered 1 through 8. A chord may be built in thirds (using every other tone) on any degree of the scale. A chord may be named for the degree of the scale or called by its letter name. The three chords superimposed on the tonic, subdominant and dominant of the major scale are those most often used. Among them they include every degree of the scale and, thus, harmonize with any simple song that stays within the key.

Sometimes the V chord is extended to include another tone which is the seventh above the root. This is called the V_7 or, in the key of C, the G_7 chord.

These three chords are found in a traditional sequence in hundreds of American folk songs. I IV (I) V($_7$) I.

Grades K – 3

- Play four even strokes on each chord (C . . . F . . . G$_7$ . . .) C . . .)
- Repeat this several times with children indicating the chord changes by raising a hand.
- Following a leader, children march to the "Cadence March."

Grades 4 – 8

- Strum each of these chords four times: C, F, G$_7$, C.
- Repeat as the students listen to the chord changes.
- Strum four times on these chords: C, F, C, G$_7$, C.
- Repeat as the students listen to the chord changes.
- Analyze the chords.

Enrichment:

- Sing "Wildwood Flower."
- Play chords for any of these songs: "Camptown Races," "Goodbye Old Paint," "Hey, Betty Martin," "Marine's Hymn," "Rock Island Line," "Sourwood Mountain," "This Land is Your Land," "Red River Valley," "Aloha Oe." See the autoharp chord chart for how to transpose chords.

Enrichment:

Encourage students to work out chords for these easy two-chord songs: "Ain't Gonna' Rain," "Bought Me a Cat," "Old Texas."

New Sounds

A STORM IN THE ROCKIES
(Tone Clusters)

Grades: 4 – 6

Focus: Creating new sounds with tone clusters.

Materials: Piano.

Procedure:

Tone clusters are collections of adjacent tones that are sounded simultaneously. They may be played with the fist, flat hands or forearm. Keys are pressed down, not struck. To sustain the aggregate of sound, depress the sostenuto (right) pedal immediately after sounding the keys.

- Demonstrate the techniques of playing on black keys; on white keys in both low and high registers; with and without the sostenuto pedal.
- Let volunteers try for effects of thunder, calm rain, etc.
- Plan a sequence of sounds to fit the progress of a storm (beginning, in progress, variations, calm).

Enrichment:

Using available melody instruments, play adjacent tones together. The blend of instrumental timbres will be interesting.

Related Activities:

Listen to *The Tides of Manaunaun* by Henry Cowell. The tone clusters in this piece suggest the movement and roar of the ocean tides.

NEW SOUNDS ON THE AUTOHARP

Grades: 4 – 8

Focus: Developing discriminating listening; Manipulation of sounds; Developing new playing techniques and understandings on the autoharp.

Materials: One or more autoharps.

Procedure:

Contemporary composers are constantly searching for new sounds. The autoharp is a good vehicle for the exploration of sounds and the techniques of producing them. By combining and alternating different sounds into patterns, children can produce their own compositions.

Producing chords on the autoharp by depressing the chord buttons is the most common way to use the autoharp. However, there are many other potential sounds to explore and organize. Here is a guide for exploring these sounds. Lead the students in examining the instrument. Record each different sound as it is produced. Let students develop their own terminology.

1 • Stroke the strings on the right side of the bars. Notice that you produce very low up to very high tones.
  • Repeat several times, letting the sounds gradually die away. Stroke upward, Stroke downward.
  • Repeat stroke, then immediately depress *all* buttons.
  • Repeat stroke, depressing one button.
  • Repeat, depressing other buttons.
  • Discuss the resulting chords.

2 • Stroke the strings on the left side of the bars. Notice that you produce very low but not very high tones.
  • Lead a discussion of string lengths and resulting sounds.

3 • Pluck each string of the lower octave. (Most autoharps have three octaves.) Notice that only selected tones are included.
  • Pluck in sequence, C̲-E-G-C̅ (C major triad)
  • Pluck in sequence, F̲-F-A-C (F major triad)
  • Pluck in sequence, G̲-G-B-D, then F (G₇ chord)
  • Depress these buttons, C-F-G₇ and C, but strum only above the lowest octave.
  • Experiment with other buttons and strums. Record all possibilities.

4   • Starting with C, pluck each string in the middle octave. These twelve tones make up the chromatic or half-tone scale.

    • Pluck each string in the higher octave.

    • Pluck the strings in a downward sequence.

5   • Pluck, in sequence, every other string in the middle octave.

    • This forms the whole-tone scale, with each tone two half-steps apart.

    • Pluck these strings in a downward sequence.

6   • In the middle octave, pluck in sequence, C-E-G-C.

    • Press the C major button. Strum the middle octave. Compare the plucked and strummed tones.

    • Repeat this with F-A-C and G-B-D.

7   • Depress the C button. Strum on the right side once and on the left side twice. This produces a very showy waltz rhythm.

    • Continue this kind of strumming with this chord sequence: C-D-F-G$_7$-C.

8   • Depress the C button. On the right side, strum the lower octave, then the middle octave, then the higher octave, pausing in between to produce another variation of the waltz rhythm.

9   • Stroke the lower octave with the thumb (away from you) (C button).

    • Stroke the middle and upper octaves with fingernails away from you to produce still another pattern of 3/4.

10   • Bounce a wooden pencil flat on the strings to the left of the bars.

    • Place a small box on the left side of the bars. Strum on the right side.

    • Depress buttons in groups of two or three at a time to produce a muffled sound.

11   • Tap the wood on the right end for a low sound.

    • Tap the wood on the other sides for higher sounds.

    • Run an eraser end of a pencil across the low strings to produce a guiro effect.

CREATING NEW SOUNDS WITH TAPE RECORDERS

Lesson One

Grades: 5 – 8

Focus: Working a reel-to-reel tape recorder; Recording the human voice at different speeds ("Old Brass Wagon").

Materials: One reel-to-reel tape recorder with three speeds.

Procedure:

Contemporary composers are using electronic instruments such as synthesizers and computers to explore the possibilities of new sounds and structures in music. However, tape recorders are readily available and offer great possibilities for experimentation with new sounds in the classroom.

- Review one verse of "The Old Brass Wagon."
- Demonstrate how to work the tape recorder (play, record, set speeds, volume).
- Set speed at 7:1/2. Record the singing of the song at 7:1/2. (A)
- Set the speed at 3:3/4 and, continuing the tape, record the song again. (B)
- Set the speed back to 7:1/2 and record the song again. (A)
- Set the speed at 1:3/4 and record the singing again. (C)
- Set the speed back to 7:1/2 and record the song once more. (A)
- Listen to the entire sequence of your newly composed rondo. (A B A C A)
- Notice that by changing the speeds, the sounds are distorted and new sounds are created.

CREATING NEW SOUNDS WITH TAPE RECORDERS

Lesson Two

Focus: Recording from one tape recorder to another; Transforming sounds, changing pitches.

Materials: Two reel-to-reel tape recorders; autoharp and/or available percussion instruments.

Procedure:

- Review the song, "Old Brass Wagon."
- Practice it with autoharp and/or percussion accompaniment.

Part 1. To transform and raise the pitch

- On tape recorder I, record "Old Brass Wagon" at *slow* speed.
- On tape recorder 1, replay material at *fast* speed while recording it on the tape recorder 2 at a *slow* speed.
- On tape recorder 2, play material at *fast* speed while recording it on tape recorder 1 at a *slow* speed.
- Continue this any number of times.

Part 2. To transform and lower the pitch

- Reverse the procedure of Part 1.

Retain your transformed sounds for the lesson on making a tape loop.

Enrichment:

Prepare other kinds of materials such as a short excerpt from a popular recording, a live performance, or natural sounds such as a series of street sounds.

CREATING NEW SOUNDS WITH TAPE RECORDERS

Lesson Three: A Tape Loop

Focus: Making and using a tape loop.

Materials: Recorded tape from previous lessons; Three tape recorders (one may be a cassette).

Procedure:

Making the Tape

- Listen to the recorded tape to find an especially interesting segment.
- From this, cut a segment large enough to fit around the two spindles on tape recorder 2.
- Splice this piece together to make a loop.
- Thread the tape loop through tape recorder 2 as you would a regular reel.
- Play the loop; it will repeat the same sounds over and over (an ostinato).

Using the Tape Loop

- Repair (splice) the original tape and rethread it on tape recorder 1.
- Set tape recorder 1 and tape recorder 2 close together.
- Play the loop and original tape simultaneously while recording them on tape recorder 3.

CREATING NEW SOUNDS WITH TAPE RECORDERS

Lesson Four

Focus: Composing a "chance" tape recorder piece; Composing a "planned" tape recorder piece.

Materials: Prepared sounds from previous lessons or newly prepared sounds.

Procedure:

Listen to the prepared sound materials, identifying possible usable segments.

A Chance Piece

- Identify the contrasting segments to be used.
- Cut several inches of each.
- Splice them together in any order. (Short lengths of unrecorded tape may be spliced in between some segments.)

A Planned Piece

- Score the composition by inches (or seconds) and kinds of sounds with a graphic representation for each sound. One plan might be
  —Explosive sounds (dots) (12")
  —Soft-high sounds (curved lines) (20")
  —Loud-low sounds (series of small rectangles) (10")
  —Mixed sounds (several symbols overlaid) (24")
- Splice the segments together as planned.
- Play the tape, checking it with your score.

THE TWELVE TONES OF THE OCTAVE

Music containing the twelve tones of the chromatic scale is not new. Chromaticism was present in the Baroque, Classical and Romantic periods. In the nineteenth century, the Romantics exploited the chromatic scale by extensive use of florid ornamentation and the cadenza.

The twentieth century tonal row system is entirely different. It is free of a home key; dissonances and consonances are tolerated equally; there is no tonic-dominant relationship; and there is no established form of resolution. In the twelve-tone technique, the order and tonal center of the major-minor system is replaced by a row or a basic set of twelve tones. The composer sets up the raw material—a row made up of each of the pitches of the chromatic scale, in any order and in any octave. Each tone may be used only once in the same order. However, after the row has been introduced, it may be used in retrograde (backwards), inversion (upside down), and/or retrograde inversion (upside down and backwards).

The easiest way to "see" this scale is to play all the black and white keys in one octave on a keyboard, on mallet bells, or on any instrument that is tuned to the twelve equal semitones.

In more complex twelve-tone music, composers sometimes set up their own variation of the rules, using repeated tones, octaves or the tones in chords. The composer's symbols are set up at the beginning of the piece to help the performer interpret the music as the composer intended it to be performed.

However, rhythm must be added to make any twelve-tone row a musical theme. The myriad of rhythm combinations, both simple and complex, that can be used with a row is one of the fascinating things about composing this kind of music.

The following lessons provide simple experiences in creating twelve-tone music. They will enable the student to develop a concept of the nature and feeling of this kind of music.

THE TWELVE TONES

Lesson One

Grades: 4 – 8

Focus: The twelve tones in sequence (chromatic scale).

Materials: Detachable resonator bells (12 bars, C to C).

Procedure:

- Twelve students each take one bar and mallet.
- Students line up so that bells are in ascending order.
- Students play each bar in order, ascending.
- Starting at the other end, students play each bar in order, descending.
- In ascending order, students play the rhythm of this phrase: "Old Mc-Don-ald had a farm, E-i, E-i, O."
- Repeat this in descending order.
- Repeat it ascending and descending.

Enrichment:

Play the rhythm of the entire song ("Old McDonald"), using the bells in any order.

A RANDOM ROW

Lesson Two

Focus: Playing and hearing a random row; Combining it with basic rhythms.

Procedure:

- Twelve students each take one bar and mallet.
- Students quickly line up with no regard to the order of the bells.
- Each student plays in turn.
- Repeat the row several times.
- Extend the line so that students may be grouped into six groups of two each with a slight space between the groups.
- Play the row again, this time accenting the first tone in each group by stamping one foot as the bar is struck. (1 – 2)
- Repeat this several times. Regroup into four groups of three.
- Students play, again accenting the first tone in each group by stamping. (1 – 2 – 3)
- End the lesson by changing places until the twelve tones are in ascending order. Play them in order once.

Enrichment:

- Regroup into three groups of four; two groups of six.
- Regroup into uneven groups such as one group of five, one group of seven; one group of six, one group of two, one group of three, and one bell alone.

A PLANNED ROW THEME

Lesson Three

Focus: Planning and building a row; Combining it with a familiar song rhythm to make a theme.

Procedure:

The row may be planned in one of several ways.

1. Use the words of a familiar song like "Hey, Betty Martin, tip-toe, tip-toe" etc.

2. Make up a word phrase "What are you doing? You're making. up new music." Then arrange the bells into a melody that seems to suit the rhythm of the words.

3. Arrange the bells in a sequence that pleases the group. Using accents (foot or percussion) on tones that are important, play the sequence in rhythm as in Lesson Two.

4. Use the rhythm of a phrase from a march like "Stars and Stripes Forever," arranging the bells into a melody.

5. The bells may be played by twelve students or they may be lined up on a table and played by one student. Alternate playing of the row forward and backward gives variety.

THE SUITE FOR PIANO

Opus 25 (1924)
by
Arnold Schoenberg

Focus: Listening to early serial music; Understanding the music.

Materials: Recordings.

Procedure:

Arnold Schoenberg, creator of the method of composing music using the twelve semi-tones, was a naturalized American citizen. Although he lived in the United States for only eighteen years, the impact of his writing and teaching was great, especially during the eight years he taught composition at the University of California at Los Angeles.

The *Suite for Piano* is one of the first pieces to be organized on the basis of a tone row. This is the basic row of the suite in its original form.

- Review the basic elements of row music.
- Discuss Schoenberg.
- Play the basic row for the *Suite for Piano*.
- Listen to the *Suite for Piano*.
- Discuss the music of Schoenberg and compare it with the music the students developed.

Enrichment:

Develop a new piece using the row from the *Suite for Piano*.

The American Heritage

CREATING AN AMERICAN MEDLEY

Grades: 4 – 8

Focus: Combining phrases of familiar American songs.

Materials: chalkboard, instruments for accompaniment, tape recorder.

Procedure:

A musical medley is a mixture of passages from various sources. Use only familiar American songs for this medley.

- Review familiar songs and instrumental pieces.
- List them on the chalkboard.
- Go through each piece and choose the most distinctive phrase or part that can be recognized without the rest of the piece.
- Experiment with sequencing the excerpts. Are the changes from one to the other too abrupt? If so, insert chords common to each song. When changing from one rhythm to another, a pause or a sustained chord sometimes prepares the listener for the new rhythm.
- Perform the music in the order outlined. Tape it.
- Evaluate the results and make any changes suggested.

Songs that might be used: "America the Beautiful," "Assembly Call," "Reveille," "Buffalo Gals," "Goodbye Old Paint," "I'm Gonna Sing," "Indian Melody," "President's March," "Stars and Stripes Forever," "Yankee Doodle."

GEORGE WASHINGTON AND THE CHERRY TREE

Grades: K – 2

Focus: Telling a short story with descriptive words and rhythmic sound effects.

Materials: Available soundmakers.

Procedure:

It is said that George Washington was a mischievous boy. One day when trying out his new axe, he chopped down his father's favorite cherry tree. When his father found out, he called George to explain. And, so the story goes, George said, "Father, I cannot tell a lie. I chopped down the cherry tree."

- Tell the story.
- Encourage the children to enlarge upon the story.
- When the story is completed to their satisfaction, explore sounds to imitate George whistling as he goes along with his axe, the sound of the axe, the tree falling, and the conclusion.
- Put the story back together with a narrator (or several story tellers) and sounds from the collected sources.

A FOURTH OF JULY PARADE
(Tune: "Hush Little Baby")

Grades: 1 – 3

Focus: Rhythm of words (accented and unaccented words); Rhyming words.

Materials: Chart paper or chalkboard.

Procedure:

One of the easiest and most satisfying ways of creating music is to add words to a familiar melody. First, choose the subject of your song. As you experiment with putting the words to the music, notice the rhythm of the words (accented and unaccented syllables). This is the first clue. The rhyming pattern is the second clue.

- Sing the words or hum the melody of "Hush Little Baby." (If the song is not familiar, delay the creation of a new song.)
- Discuss parades. Make a list of what you might see in a parade.
- The new verses are going to be about a Fourth of July parade.
- Sing the following verses with exaggerated accents to set the rhythm and rhyming patterns.

(1) *Sit* yourself *down* and *lis*ten to *me*;
    I'm gonna' *tell* you *what* you'll *see.*
(2) Down the street comes the big parade;
    See the drummer with the drum he played.
(3) Trotting horses come in sight;
    Swaying left, then swaying right.

Notice that the last words rhyme. After an idea has been offered, help the children with words that rhyme. (Experiment with several consonants before the vowel in the last word—me, see, free, tea, he, she.)

Hush Little Baby

Southern Folk Song

Enrichment:

Some of the original verses may be used in another situation.

(1) Hush little baby, Don't say a word,
    Papa's gonna' buy you a mocking bird.
(2) If that mocking bird won't sing,
    Papa's gonna' buy you a diamond ring.
(3) If that diamond ring turns brass,
    Papa's gonn' buy you a looking glass.
(4) If that looking glass gets broke,
    Papa's gonna buy you a billy goat.

AMERICA THE BEAUTIFUL

(Word Pictures)

Grades: 4 – 8

Focus: Creating word pictures of local scenes in music.

Materials: Chalkboard or erasable chart.

Procedure:

The words are by Katharine Lee Bates, who was a professor of English at Wellesley College. She wrote them after a visit to Pike's

Peak in Colorado. From the mountain she could see all the things mentioned in the song. This poem expresses her feeling about the beauty of America. The song is made up of word pictures: "amber waves of grain," "purple mountain majesties," "fruited plain."

Part I.

- Read the words as a poem.
- Discuss the meaning of all the words.
- Students read the words with expression (alone, together, silently, as a chant).
- Sing the song.

Part 2.

- Discuss the beauty of nature in your locality.
- Record students' suggestions on the chalkboard.
- Students fit their descriptions into the melody of the verse. (Note the rhyming scheme.)

America the Beautiful

Katherine Lee Bates   Samuel A. Ward

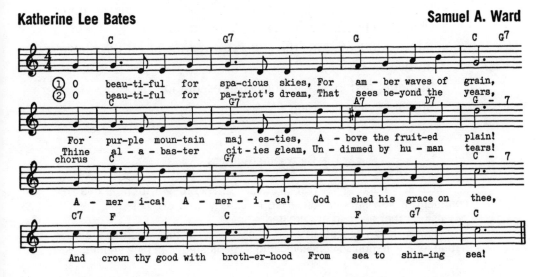

THE GETTYSBURG ADDRESS
(Background Music)

The battle at Gettysburg, Pennsylvania on July 1–3, 1863, became the turning point of the Civil War. Later, when this battlefield was dedicated as a soldiers' cemetery, many notable people came to make speeches. President Lincoln's famous address is considered a classic of oratory and an outstanding expression of democratic principles.

Grades: 5– 8

Focus: Choric and/or solo reading of The Gettysburg Address with background music; The role preparation of background music.

Materials: Familiar patriotic songs; Tape recorder.

Procedure:

Background music is used to enhance or emphasize spoken words. It must never detract from or overpower the recitation. The music is selected for its compatibility with the subject matter, its rhythm, and general mood. It may be vocal or instrumental and may be fragments of compositions.

- Students read The Gettysburg Address together.
- Discuss the setting and reason for the address.
- Make a list of familiar songs and instrumental pieces from which to choose the background music.
- As one student reads the address, experiment with available music.
- Students perform their finished presentation; tape it.
- Students evaluate their efforts.

The Gettysburg Address

Four score and seven years ago our fathers brought forth on this continent, a new nation, conceived in Liberty, and dedicated to the proposition that all men are created equal.

Now we are engaged in a great civil war, testing whether that nation, or any nation so conceived and so dedicated, can long endure.

We are met on a great battlefield of that war. We have come to dedicate a portion of that field, as a final resting-place for those who here
gave their lives that that nation might live. It is altogether fitting and
proper that we should do this.

But, in a larger sense, we can not dedicate — we can not consec-
rate — we can not hallow — this ground. The brave men, living and
dead, who struggled here, have consecrated it, far above our poor
power to add or detract. The world will little note, nor long remember,
what we say here, but it can never forget what they did here. It is for us
the living, rather to be dedicated here to the unfinished work which
they who fought here have thus far so nobly advanced. It is rather for
us to be here dedicated to the great task remaining before us—that
from these honored dead we take increased devotion to that cause for
which they gave the last full measure of devotion — that we here
highly resolve that these dead shall not have died in vain — that this
nation, under God, shall have a new birth of freedom — and that
government of the people, by the people, for the people, shall not
perish from the earth.

****

SUMMING UP

The heritage of American music and the basic aspects of
musicianship are combined in this book. By means of prepared
lesson plans, teachers can involve children in the performance of
a representative sampling of American music and, at the same
time, develop basic musicianship according to the experiences,
abilities and age levels of the children.

When young Americans become aware of their musical
heritage they take pride in it. When they are actively involved
in performing American music they enjoy it, begin to understand it and find out how extensive and remarkable it is.

When children in other countries have the opportunity to
hear American music, sing American songs, dance American
dances, and, perhaps, learn to play an American instrument,
they learn to respect the great American musical heritage.

There are many kinds of American music presented in the
lessons in this book—inspirational; patriotic; traditional folk
music of different kinds; fun songs; dance music; ethnic music—
the gift immigrants bring with them; music for band, orchestra,

piano and other solo instruments; chamber music; and, finally, the important and ever-changing "pop" music. Music for these lessons has been carefully selected to present various styles of American music, not only in the tonic-dominant tradition but also in the more sophisticated twentieth century bases like serial and electronic.

When children become aware that music is more than random sounds they become interested. When they focus on specific aspects of music related to their immediate musical performance, they establish basic concepts of how sounds are organized into music. When they develop basic music skills they understand music and are able to delve into new music independently and make music part of their lives.

The development of musicianship begins with the establishment of concepts of pitch (melody), duration (rhythm), harmony, and timbre (quality of sounds). The development of music skills, using these concepts in the performance of music, is gradual. It begins with childrens' first musical experiences and continues throughout all subsequent experiences. Each lesson in this book focuses on a specific musical concept and/or skill.

The exploration and understanding of the American musical heritage is enhanced by the basic understanding of the music itself. These lessons help teachers and, through them, children, begin that fascinating journey of exploration.

Index

A

B

C

D

H

I

J

K

L

M

N

O

S

T

U

V

W

Y